POKER TALK
Learn How to Talk Poker Like a Pro

About the Author

Avery Cardoza is the world's foremost authority on gambling, a multimillion-selling author of 21 books, and the publisher of the acclaimed national gambling lifestyle magazine, *Avery Cardoza's Player*. His poker books include *How to Play Winning Poker, Poker Talk, The Basics of Winning Hold'em Poker, The Basics of Winning Poker*, and the upcoming title, *Crash Course in Beating Texas Hold'em Poker*.

He is a frequent money-winner and regular player in the high stakes poker tournaments seen on television. Cardoza has crippled the stacks of, or eliminated, more than a dozen world champions from major tournament competitions.

POKER TALK
Learn How to Talk Poker Like a Pro

AVERY CARDOZA

CARDOZA
PUBLISHING

Cardoza Publishing is the foremost gaming publisher in the world with a library of more than 175 up-to-date and easy-to-read books and strategies. These authoritative works are written by the top experts in their fields and with more than 8,500,000 books in print, represent the best-selling and most popular gaming books anywhere.

FIRST EDITION

Library of Congress Catalog Card Number: 2005920571
ISBN: 1-58042-168-7
Front cover art by John Higgins; interior cartoons by Jon Carter

Visit our website—www.cardozapub.com—or write for a full list of Cardoza books and advanced strategies.

CARDOZA PUBLISHING
P.O. Box 1500, Cooper Station, New York, NY 10276
Phone (800)577-WINS
email: cardozapub@aol.com
www.cardozapub.com

—*To Gary Bauer*

My wise and odd friend, author of the unpublished *Roasted Heart*, appreciates language more than anyone I've ever met, so this collection of poker patois is dedicated to him.

Acknowledgements

A word of thanks goes out to Nolan Dalla for looking over the manuscript and providing input, Jim Mauro for useful guidance, and Michael Wiesenberg, the main editor whose sharp eye was greatly helpful in maintaining the accuracy of the text and contributing to make this a better book. Being the author of a poker dictionary himself, *The Official Dictionary of Poker*, Michael was uniquely qualified for the task. Also thanks to Dustin York for a beautiful presentation of the layout.

I was fortunate to be working with two artists who greatly enhanced the look of the book, John Higgins, who drew the cover image and Jon Carter, who created the cartoons seen throughout the text.

Table of Contents

—◆—

Introduction

Get ready for the most fascinating and fabulous collection of colorful poker words, phrases, and poker-speak ever assembled. This chip chatter is the real deal, the actual talk bandied around the poker table. No longer is it enough to know how to walk the walk in poker, you need to know how to talk the talk!

This fun book will show you what it means to go all in on a rainbow flop with pocket rockets and get it cracked by cowboys, put a bad beat on a calling station when he misses his runner-runner on the river, and go over the top of a producer fishing with a gutshot to win a big dime.

When your card-playing friends start talking poker, you'll be one step ahead, armed with this great collection of more than 2,000 definitions. Throw a feeler bet into that conversation and you'll have those railbirds wondering what *you* are talking about.

I hope you enjoy this book!

— Avery Cardoza

Cross-References

A term in SMALL CAPITALS is a cross-reference. That is, more information can be found at the referenced term. A term in italics is either an example of usage or a term that is listed elsewhere but that does not have additional information.

The Genesis of Poker Talk

This book took root in my head while I was editing Doyle Brunson's *Super System 2* in mid-2004. As I sifted through the chapters of such poker greats as Mike Caro, Lyle Berman, Johnny Chan, Daniel Negreanu, Todd Brunson, Jennifer Harman, Crandall Addington, and of course, Doyle himself, I was struck not only by the richness of their language, but that it was *another* language.

For some ungodly reason, I started collecting words and phrases from live play and tournaments and began this project, as if my typical 100-120-hour work week was not sufficient enough work. I also pored through poker literature and soaked up the colorful language of T. J. Cloutier and other road gamblers until I was comfortable that a full collection of this arcane patois was assembled. Before I knew it, a project I had guessed might top out at several hundred listings grew to thousands. *I had no idea.*

The result, finished between other deadlines in the dog days of summer in "the sweatbox," my sweltering unventilated and non-air-conditioned New York City loft with "cooling" poker trips to Las Vegas and its 115-degree heat, allows me to truthfully say that I sweated out this dictionary to make it the best I could. If there are terms you think should be added to future editions, email them to me at cardozapoker@aol.com.

Hand Ranking and Basic Poker Expressions

Here is a quick guide to poker hand rankings as well as the most common forms of announcing a hand. Generally, a player simply turns over his hand at the show-down and lets the *cards speak*, particularly in a game run by a house dealer. But often, particularly when discussing a hand, he may simply state the hand's value. For example, "I have a pair of nines" or "I have a flush."

These are the rankings of high poker hands, from worst to best:

high card: A hand that has no higher-ranking combinations, such as a pair, two pair, or better; basically five odd cards. Such a hand is named by its highest-ranking card. For example, 3-9-K-7-10 is a *king-high* hand. Also called *no pair*.

one pair: Two cards of equal rank. For example, 5-5-8-J-K, would be announced as *fives, a pair of fives*, or *fives with a king kicker*. In the last case, a player might specify the highest side card in case another player has a pair of fives, in which case the side card would be used to determine the highest-ranking hand.

two pair: Two pairs and an odd card. For example, 6-6-J-J-2. Two pair hands often include the word "and," "up," or "over" after the higher pair, with the second, smaller pair usually listed second. For example, A-A-7-K-K would commonly be announced as *aces over kings*, *aces and kings*, or simply *aces up*. With the "and" form, a hand like 6-6-4-4-J is typically expressed with the larger pair first, *sixes and fours*.

three of a kind: Three cards of equal rank and two odds cards. For example, Q-Q-Q-7-J, announced as *three queens*, *a set of queens*, or *trip queens*.

straight: Five cards in sequence. For example, 8-9-10-J-Q of mixed suits, announced as *straight* or *queen-high straight*. In the latter expression, a player might specify the highest card in case another player has a straight, in which case the highest card held determines the winning hand. A straight does not "wrap" around the ace, so, for example, Q-K-A-2-3 of mixed suits is not a straight, but simply an ace-high hand, and an A-2-3-4-5 is considered a five-high straight, with the ace counting as a low card and losing to any straight containing a 6 or higher.

flush: Five cards of the same suit (not in sequence). For example, 3♦ 5♦ 9♦ 10♦ K♦, announced as *flush*, *diamond flush* (while the suit value is always irrelevant in poker, players often announce it), *king-high diamond flush*, or *king-high flush*. In the latter form, a player might specify the highest card to determine the winning hand in case another player also has a flush.

full house: Three of a kind plus a pair. For example, 5-5-5-9-9, announced as *a full house*, *full*, *boat*, *full boat*, *filled up*, *fives full*, *fives full of nines*.

straight flush: Five cards in sequence all in the same suit. For example, 3-4-5-6-7, all spades, announced as *straight flush* or *7-high straight flush*. Indication of top card of a straight flush is usually unnecessary as it is extremely rare that two players would hold a straight flush in the same hand. Mentioning the suit as part of the hand has no relevance, though some players do specify the rank of the top card and the suit.

royal flush: A-K-Q-J-10 of the same suit, technically a straight flush topped by an ace, the rarest and best hand possible in poker. Announced as *royal flush* or *royal flush in hearts*, the suit value expressed just to give added emphasis to the beauty of a hand that is seen only a few times, if ever, in a lifetime of play.

The Talk

♣: Symbol used for a card in the suit of clubs.

♦: Symbol used for a card in the suit of diamonds.

♥: Symbol used for a card in the suit of hearts.

♠: Symbol used for a card in the suit of spades.

A: Symbol used in written text for an ace in any suit.

a-b-c player: A player whose by-the-book strategy makes him somewhat predictable.

above the curve: In a tournament, having more than the average number of chips.

absolute nuts: The best hand possible based on the cards on board.

ace: **1.** In high poker, the best and highest card. **2.** In ACE-TO-FIVE low poker (as opposed to DEUCE-TO-SEVEN), the best and *lowest* card. Also *bullet*, *rocket*, *spike*, and many other names.

ace-any: An ace with any card.

ace-face: An ace with either a jack, queen, or king.

ace high: A hand that has no pairs or higher combinations and whose highest card is an ace.

ace-high: A specific hand in which the ace is the highest card, as *ace-high straight*, *ace-high flush*, or simply an *ace-high hand*.

ace kicker: Having an ace as a side card to a hand such as a PAIR or TWO PAIR.

ace-killers: Hands that render aces, powerful starting cards in hold'em, second-best.

ace-little: An ace accompanied by a small card, usually a 7 or smaller.

aces: A PAIR of aces.

aces and eights: The cards held by Wild Bill Hickok when he was shot dead in a poker game in the early 1800s. Often called DEAD MAN'S HAND.

aces and spaces: A pair of aces and unmatched cards of mixed suits, such as Omaha starting cards of A-A-8-5 or hold'em board cards of A-A-10-7-2, such that the additional cards don't easily form straights or flushes.

ace in the hole: 1. An ace as a downcard in a stud game. **2.** A powerful secret weapon.

ace-to-five: A variation of low poker in which the best and lowest card is the ace, straights and flushes don't count, and the best hand is A-2-3-4-5; also known as *ace-to-five lowball.* Compare with DEUCE-TO-SEVEN LOWBALL, in which the ace is always high.

ace up the sleeve: 1. An ace that a cheater has concealed in the sleeve of his shirt. **2.** By extension, a secret weapon, sometimes an unfair one.

act: To bet, raise, fold, or check.

action: 1. Betting, raising, checking, or folding. **2.** A player who bets and raises aggressively or a game with frequent betting and raising. "Fernando is an action player." "This is an action game."

action flop: In hold'em or Omaha, a flop that tends to induce a lot of bets and calls.

action game: A game with much betting and raising, as opposed to a PASSIVE GAME.

"Action on me": Announcement by a player acknowledging it is his turn to act.

active: A hand or player still in contention for the pot.

active hand: A hand that is still LIVE, that is, not folded and still in contention for the pot.

active player: A player still in competition for the pot.

add on: Purchase additional chips, an option available at the end of the first few rounds of play in ADD-ON TOURNAMENTS.

add-on: Chips purchased by adding on, or the cost of those chips.

add-on tournament: A tournament that allows players a final purchase of a specified amount of additional chips, usually at the end of the first few rounds of play. See SINGLE ADD-ON TOURNAMENT, DOUBLE ADD-ON TOURNAMENT.

advance action button: In online poker, a button that permits a player to select a play (bet, raise, fold, raise any, etc.) before it is his turn to act.

advantage: A situation with a winning expectation.

advertise: Intentionally play weak cards to the showdown to misrepresent one's playing style or skill level, or bluff in a situation in which one is likely to be called, setting the stage for trapping opponents on future hands.

against the odds: A hand or situation that, mathematically, is favored to lose.

aggressive: 1. A player who frequently bets and raises. **2.** When applied to a game, frequent betting and raising, and thus implying one with big pots.

◆

ahead: 1. Winning money. **2.** Having the best hand at the moment. **3.** Acting before another player or players.

Ajax: In hold'em, hole cards of A-J.

all black: Consisting of only black cards in one's hand or on the board, that is, spades and clubs.

all in: When a player has all his chips committed to a pot.

all red: Consisting of only red cards in one's hand or on the board, that is, hearts and diamonds.

all the way: Staying in a pot, calling opponents' bets and raises until the showdown.

a.m.: DAY SHIFT.

ammunition: Chips.

Anaconda: A seven-card stud variation in which players select cards to pass to other players, and then expose some of those cards in similar fashion to the dealing of seven-card stud. Also, *pass the trash.*

◆

ALL IN: WHEN A PLAYER HAS ALL HIS CHIPS COMMITTED TO A POT.

announce: 1. Call out a betting action. **2.** Make a poorly disguised or imprudent bet that gives away the strength of one's hand.

ante: 1. Mandatory bet placed into the pot by all players before the cards are dealt; compare with BLIND. **2.** Put such a bet in the pot.

"Ante up": A call for a player or players to put their antes into the pot.

anything opens: A high draw poker variation that has no opening requirement, as opposed to a game such as JACKS OR BETTER, in which a holding of a minimum of a pair of jacks is required.

around back: Sitting in LATE POSITION.

around front: Sitting in EARLY POSITION.

ATM: A player who supplies money to other players through his losses. "I've been taking his money all night. He's my ATM."

attack the blind: Raise with the intention of forcing out blinds and "stealing" their chips.

automatic bluff: A situation in which the correct strategy is to bluff regardless of the strength of one's cards.

automatic fold: 1. A hand so poor that it should be surrendered against any bet. **2.** In online poker, a preselected option—before one's turn to act—to fold a hand.

average stack size: In a tournament, the average number of chips remaining per player, calculated by dividing the number of remaining players into the original starting field and multiplying the result by the per-player starting chip total. For example, if 50 players remain out of a starting field of 200, and each started with $10,000 in chips, then the average chip count would be $40,000.

Avery Cardoza's Player: A lifestyle magazine devoted to poker and gambling.

baby: A low card. In ACE-TO-FIVE lowball, usually ace through 5.

back: 1. STAKE. **2.** Being in LATE POSITION. Also, BACK POSITION, AROUND BACK.

backdoor: Make an unlikely straight or flush late in a hand by catching successive cards on the last rounds of play. For example, in hold'em, if a player flops J-10-3 to his A-J hand, then catches a king and queen on the TURN and RIVER, he has *backdoored a straight.*

backdoor flush: Make an unlikely flush by catching two successive suited cards.

backdoor straight: Make an unlikely straight by catching two successive cards.

backed up: 1. Having the second pair in a two-pair hand, as *jacks backed up by tens.* **2.** In flop and stud games, having a pair in the downcards.

backer: An individual who finances a player in return for a cut of the profit. "T.J. Cloutier can find a backer for any tournament he wants to play."

back in: Win a pot with a hand different than what was originally played for, for example, in hold'em, to start with a pair and end with a BACKDOOR STRAIGHT.

back into a hand: Make a hand that originally wasn't being drawn to. See BACKDOOR.

back position: One of the last players to act in a betting round; LATE POSITION.

backraise: A reraise from a player who originally called in a round, but responded to a raise by reraising.

backside: LATE POSITION.

back-to-back: 1. Any two successive hands or events. **2.** Specifically two cards of the same rank or suit or hands of like nature, drawn right after one another. **3.** A pair in the first two cards dealt.

backup: In low or HIGH-LOW poker, an extra low card that helps prevent a low hand from getting COUNTERFEITED (duplicated) on the board and becoming useless. For example, in Omaha, with a hand of A-2-6-J and a board of 3-7-K, the 6 serves as a backup for low in case an ace or deuce gets dealt on the turn or river (thus allowing the other two low cards in the hand to combine with the three on the board to form a qualified low.) Also BACKUP DRAW, *secondary draw.*

backup draw: A drawing hand that also has a less likely draw possible that may come through if the primary draw doesn't fill. Also, *secondary draw*.

bad action: A game with little betting and small pots.

bad beat: A loss with a hand that was heavily favored to win.

bad beat jackpot: See JACKPOT.

bad game: A game that is likely to be unprofitable due to skilled opposition or a waste of time due to small stakes.

bad luck: Misfortune that seems to occur more frequently than random chance would suggest.

bad one: A dealt card that either doesn't improve one's hand or likely makes an opponent's hand better or appear to be better.

bad percentage play: A mathematically unsound play, one that will not show a profit in the long run.

bad run: A series of plays or sessions that end unfavorably. Also, *losing streak*. Opposite of *good run* or *good streak*.

bait: A small bet or raise made to suck an opponent deeper into a hand or to encourage a raise.

bank: 1. The person, group, or place that holds the money in a game or books the action. **2.** A player's BANKROLL. **3.** Finance another player. **4.** To make money as in *to make bank* **5:** A place where money is kept

bankroll: 1. The total amount of money a player has designated for the purposes of playing poker or actually has on his person to gamble with. **2.** Lend money to or finance a player.

bankroll buster: A hand that, if played, can devastate either a player's own chip stack or that of an opponent.

barred: Temporarily or permanently excluded from play, usually due to disruptive, rude, or unacceptable behavior. Also, *eighty-sixed*.

Baskin-Robbins: In hold'em, hole cards of A-3 (3-A); named for the 31 flavors of the ice cream brand.

BB: BIG BLIND; used in written text and online poker room chat.

◆

be dealt in: Be active in a poker hand; literally, have cards dealt to one's position.

beat: 1. Have a better hand, to win. **2.** Win more money or finish in a better position in a tournament or competition than someone else. **3.** Losing a hand that was a big favorite. See BAD BEAT.

beat into the pot: Call a bet so rapidly (usually implying a superior, winning hand), that it's as if the call of the bet got into the pot before the bettor's wager. "James bet all-in and Hamster beat him into the pot with his full house."

beat the board: In hold'em and Omaha, have a hand higher than the community cards; in seven-card stud, have a hand higher than another player's upcards. Often used in the negative. "I didn't call the bet because I couldn't beat the board."

beer hand: In hold'em, hole cards of 7-2 (the worst possible starting cards).

before the flop: In hold'em and Omaha, the action that occurs on the first betting round (when players have starting cards, but before the three-card FLOP is dealt).

---

behind: 1. Acting or being in position to act after a particular player; being in LATE POSITION. **2.** Having a lesser holding than an opponent at some point during the play of a hand.

being there: Having a hand that is already made and will probably win. "If you're there, you can push hard at your opponents."

belly buster: INSIDE STRAIGHT.

below the curve: In a tournament, having less than the average number of chips.

berry patch: A game with players ripe for the picking, that is, players who will probably lose their money.

best hand: The leading or winning hand.

best of it: 1. Having a better hand than opponents in a situation, one that will be profitable in the long run. Often part of the phrase *have, get,* or *take the best of it.* **2.** Having a winning hand.

◆

bet: 1. A wager; often specifically the chips or money placed in a pot. "Two hundred, is that your bet?" **2.** In limit poker, a one-unit wager of the current betting limit. For example, in the first round of a $2/$4 game, if one player raises to $4 and the next player puts in $6, raising it $2 more, the house dealer might announce "Three bets."

bet at the flop: Make a bet on the FLOP.

bet at the pot: Make a bet.

bet blind: Make a bet made without looking at one's cards. A bet so made is called a BLIND BET. Also *bet in the dark*.

bet down to the felt: Bet all one's chips.

bet for value: 1. Make a wager on a hand believed to be superior with the intention of getting callers and building the pot.

bet in the dark: See BET BLIND.

◆

———◆———

bet into: Bet at a player who bet or raised on a previous round, or one who shows strength on a hand in other ways (for example, staying PAT in draw poker). "Pairing his door card on fourth street, Max bet into me."

bet into a dry pot: See DRY POT.

bet limit: 1. The maximum bet size allowable in a game. Sometimes shortened to just *limit*. **2.** The betting increments of a LIMIT GAME.

bet out: 1. Make an opening bet in a round in which there is no FORCED BET. "He bet out on the flop." **2.** Bet in an emphatic manner.

bet out of turn: ACT on a hand before it is one's turn to play. This is either a breach of poker etiquette or an outright violation, depending on the rules in a given game.

bet size: 1. The dollar or chip amount of the wager being made. **2.** The STAKES of a game.

bet the farm: Make a huge bet, often all of one's bankroll on a single wager or hand.

———◆———

bet the limit: Bet the maximum allowed in POT- or SPREAD-LIMIT games.

bet the pot: Make a bet equal to the amount already in the pot in POT- and NO-LIMIT games.

betting limit: See LIMIT.

betting stakes: The amount of money required to make a minimum and maximum bet and raise.

bettor: 1. A player making, or one who has made, a bet. **2.** A player.

bicycle: In ACE-TO-FIVE lowball games, A-2-3-4-5, the best possible hand. Also, *wheel*, *bike*.

big: Short for BIG BLIND or big blind bet.

big bet: The larger bet in LIMIT poker, that is, the second level in a two-tier structure), as opposed to LITTLE BET. For example, the $10 bet in a $5/$10 game. Also, *double bet*.

big bet game: 1. POT- or NO-LIMIT game. **2.** Any game played for high stakes.

big blind: 1. The larger of two FORCED BLIND bets in flop games such as hold'em and Omaha, posted before the cards are dealt by the player two seats to the left of the BUTTON. Compare to SMALL BLIND. **2.** The player occupying this position.

big bobtail: A four card straight-flush, a nonstandard hand sometimes given value in private poker games; it ranks higher than a FULL HOUSE and lower than FOUR OF A KIND.

big-buy-in tournament: A tournament that costs $1,000 or more to enter. Also *large buy-in tournament.*

big card: 1. In high poker, usually a queen, king, or ace, and sometimes a jack. **2.** In low poker, usually a 9 or higher, cards that cannot be part of a low hand in 8-OR-BETTER games. **3.** In low poker games without a QUALIFIER, cards that are relatively high. Compare to LITTLE CARD, MEDIUM CARD.

big dime: $10,000.

big dog: A large underdog; that is, a situation in which a hand or player is unlikely to win.

big field: In a tournament, a large number of players (referring to at least several hundred).

big-field tournament: A tournament of more than 200 players.

big flop: A FLOP that gives a player a BIG HAND or a flop that contains high cards.

big full: In hold'em, the highest possible FULL HOUSE given the cards exposed on the board. For example, with a board of K-K-J-6-5, a player having a king and a jack has a *big full* of kings over jacks. Compare with SMALL FULL.

big game: The main game in a cardroom or the one with the highest stakes. "I think Doyle, Chip, and Lyle are still playing the big game."

big hand: 1. A strong poker hand, one well positioned to win. **2.** In high-low games, a hand competing for the high end of the pot.

big kicker: A side card to a PAIR or SET (or rarely, QUADS) that is relatively large; usually a king or ace.

big limit: LARGE LIMIT.

big nickel: $5,000.

big pair: A PAIR of jacks or higher.

big player: A player who gambles for high stakes.

big score: To win a large amount of money.

big slick: In hold'em, hole cards of A-K.

bike: BICYCLE.

bird dog: A person who attracts players to a poker game, or who scouts out other games.

bite: RAKE.

BK: Bankrupt.

black: **1.** A hand or board consisting of only black cards—spades and clubs. *He thought his pre-flop pocket cowboys were good until I turned over my black ace.* **2.** $100 chip (black in most casinos).

black chip: $100 chip.

blank: A card that doesn't appear to help anyone. Also, *brick, rag.*

bleed: 1. Steadily lose money. "I've been bleeding for hours."
2. Steadily win money from an opponent or game. "He's been bleeding the game all day."

blind: 1. A mandatory bet made before the cards are dealt by the player or players immediately to the button's left. Typical blinds are BIG BLIND, SMALL BLIND, sometimes WINNER BLIND. Compare to ANTE. **2.** The player making that bet.

blind bet: 1. A forced bet made before the cards are dealt. See BLIND.
2. A bet made without looking at one's cards. See BET BLIND.

blinded out: Having lost all one's chips, or a majority of them, to the forced antes and blind bets, that is, without playing hands; what happens to a player who repeatedly folds hands and loses his chips by attrition.

blind game: A game with BLINDS.

blocky: In hold'em, hole cards of 6-3.

blow back: Lose back winnings in a game because a player has stayed too long instead of quitting.

bluff: 1. Bet aggressively with an inferior hand, one unlikely to win if called, to cause opponents to fold better hands, thus making the bluffer a winner by default. **2.** A bet so made.

bluff at the pot: BLUFF.

bluffer: 1. A player who bets aggressively with weak cards to intimidate opponents into folding. **2.** A player who does this often.

board: 1. The COMMUNITY CARDS in FLOP GAMES. **2.** A player's upcards in stud games. **3.** SIGN-UP BOARD. "Are you in a game?" "I'm on the board."

board cards: 1. The COMMUNITY CARDS in FLOP GAMES. **2.** A player's upcards in stud games.

board lock: In any game featuring open cards, having the best hand possible at the moment based on those exposed cards. Also, the NUTS.

boat: FULL HOUSE. Also, FULL BOAT.

bobtail: A four-card straight or flush.

bonus: A sum of money paid to the holder of a very powerful hand, usually aces full or higher. Also *premium, royalty*.

book a loser: Have a losing session.

borderline: A marginal decision, one that has no clear-cut mathematical advantage or disadvantage.

boss hand: The best hand.

both ends: 1. BOTH WAYS. **2.** A straight draw that could be filled at either end, such as a 3-4-5-6, which can be filled by either a 2 or a 7.

both ways: In HIGH-LOW games, having cards that put one in contention for both the best high and best low hand.

bottom end of a straight: IGNORANT END OF A STRAIGHT.

bottom pair: In hold'em and Omaha, a pair formed by combining a hole card with the lowest BOARD CARD.

bottom two pair: In hold'em and Omaha, two pair formed by combining hole cards with the two lowest BOARD CARDS.

bottom wrap: In Omaha, a draw to the low end of a straight on a hand with more than eight cards that will fill the straight. For example, with hole cards of 6-4-3-Q and a flop of Q-7-5, any 8, 6, 4, or 3 makes a straight. Compare with TOP WRAP.

bounty: In a tournament, a bonus given to players who knock out specified opponents.

bounty hunter: In a BOUNTY TOURNAMENT, a player who concentrates on knocking out opponents for a cash prize.

bounty tournament: A tournament in which prizes are given to players who knock out either specific high-profile opponents or any opponents.

BR: Bankroll.

bracelet: The gold bracelet given to the winner of a World Series of Poker event. Also, *gold bracelet.*

break: 1. A cessation of play or time out in a game. **2.** The time between rounds in a tournament when play halts and players can take bathroom, smoking, or food breaks, as time allows. **3.** BREAK A HAND. "He broke the 8 and beat my 7." **4.** BREAK A PLAYER.

break a hand: In draw poker variations, to discard a card that forms a good hand—rendering it worthless—in hopes of drawing cards that will form a superior hand. For example, in ACE-TO-FIVE, a player with 9-4-3-2-A against a pat hand may think his opponent has a 7 or an 8, making his 9-high hand a potential loser. He might break the hand, that is, discard the 9, and hope to catch a 5, 6, or 7 for a stronger low.

break a player: To bankrupt an opponent by winning all his chips

break down: 1. In a tournament, disperse the players at one table for assignment to other tables. **2.** Change larger denomination chips for smaller ones. Opposite of COLOR UP. **3.** Lose one's composure and play stupidly; go ON TILT.

---

break even: Gamble and have the same bankroll as when one started, that is, show neither profit nor loss.

break-even: A play or situation in which, in the long run, neither profits or losses are expected.

break it down: Separate chips by denomination and then by stacks so that the chip amount can be verified. This is often requested by players when opponents make large bets in no-limit games or done automatically by dealers when big chip stacks are bet.

break off: 1. Catch a bad card that considerably weakens a hand. **2.** BREAK A HAND, for example, *he broke off the 8 and made a wheel*.

break someone: Win all of an opponent's money in a hand, series of hands, or session, such that he is broke or near-broke.

brick: A worthless card that appears to help no player. Also, *blank, rag, rock*.

bring-in (bet): 1. A forced bet that the holder of the high or low card, depending on the variation, must make on the first round of play in seven-card stud and some other variations. **2.** The amount required to open betting. For example, in a no-limit game, the *bring-in* is usually the size of the big blind. Thus, in a game with a small blind of $5 and a big blind of $10, the bring-in is $10.

bring it in: 1. Start the betting. **2.** PULL IT IN.

Broadway: Ace-high STRAIGHT, that is, 10-J-Q-K-A of mixed suits.

Broderick Crawford: In hold'em, hole cards of 10-4; in lowball, the hand 10-4-3-2-A. Named after the actor in *Highway Patrol*, a popular 1950s television show, who often said "10-4," an acknowledgment code, into his police radio.

broken board: In hold'em, a board with no pairs, and no good straight or flush possibilities.

broken game: A game of poker that has been disbanded.

bubble: In a tournament, the point at which all remaining players will win money except for the next player to get eliminated. For example, with 37 players remaining and 36 places paid, that 37th place is the *bubble*.

bug: 1. In some draw poker variations, a joker with limited wild card potential. It can be the fifth card to complete a straight, flush, or straight flush, or as an ace only to form two, three, four, or five ace hands. It cannot be used for any other purpose. So, for example, two kings plus the joker is just two kings and an ace. In ACE-TO-FIVE, it becomes the lowest unmatched card in the hand. **2.** A cheating device attached beneath a poker table to hold cards.

build a game around: Start a new game when a particularly key player or pool of players, usually losing ones, are available for play.

bullets: Aces.

bully: Bet and raise aggressively with the intention of intimidating opponents and causing them to fold.

bumble bee: A chip with yellow and black markings.

---

bump: Raise. "I'll bump that bet $25."

buried: 1. A card placed deeply in the pack. **2.** A downcard. **3.** A player who has incurred heavy losses. "Dino lost every pot he played in the $10/$20 game last night. He got buried." **4.** Two cards of equal rank as downcards in stud or flop games. "He had buried aces."

buried card: Downcard in a stud or flop game, said to be *buried* since no opponent can see its value.

burn: Take a card out of play, usually by discarding it face-down. "The dealer burned the first card before dealing."

burn and turn: Take a card out of play and then deal.

burn card: A card that is removed and taken out of play, usually off the top of the deck or before additional cards are dealt, as a matter of procedure (used as a precaution against accidental exposure or cheating).

bust: 1. Lose all one's chips or money. **2.** Lose with a hand. **3.** Not complete a straight or flush draw.

bust a player: Get all a player's chips and eliminate him from play.

busted: 1. To get caught bluffing. **2.** To lose all one's money. **3.** A promising hand that doesn't improve or that gets devalued by a poor draw, as a *busted flush*.

busted hand: A hand that does not improve and thus has little value, such as a four-card straight draw that doesn't complete to form the straight. *The 7 of clubs on the river busted my heart flush draw.*

bust hand: A hand with almost no winning chances.

bust out: 1. Lose, usually going broke, in a session. **2.** Exit a tournament. "He busted out on the bubble."

bust-out joint: A cardroom known to have cheaters or cheating.

button: 1. The player occupying the dealer position who, in games with BLINDS, goes last in all rounds except the first. **2.** The physical disk, often plastic and labeled "dealer," that indicates the dealer position. **3.** A disk with a similar function, as a KILL BUTTON.

POKER TALK

"button is dead": Announcement that the BUTTON position is not occupied (due to the player who had been the button busting out on the previous hand).

"button moved": Announcement (by a player or dealer) that the dealer button has moved clockwise one spot and is now in the correct position.

buy: 1. Bet or raise with inferior cards so that opponents will fold; often part of the phrase *buy the pot*. **2.** Call a bet so that another card can be seen. "Sara bought another card to see if she would make the straight." **3.** Receive cards, usually implying good ones, on the DRAW in DRAW POKER. "Foster bought three sixes on the draw." **4.** Purchase more chips.

buy-in: 1. The amount of money a player exchanges for chips to begin a poker session. **2.** The minimum amount of chips required to enter a game. Also, *change-in*.

buy the pot: See BUY. "Big J pushed in a pot-sized bet hoping to buy the pot."

c: Symbol for clubs in written text. For example, 8c is the 8♣.

cage: The area, often behind security bars in casinos (hence the name), where money is exchanged for chips or chips for money. Also *cashier's cage, window*.

California bible: Deck of cards; also called *California prayer book, railroad bible*.

California draw: The form of DRAW POKER that used to be common in California cardrooms. As a limit game, it was usually played with antes and JACKS OR BETTER as the opening requirement; as a no-limit game, it was usually played with blinds and players could open with any cards, that is, no OPENERS were required.

California lowball: ACE-TO-FIVE with a BUG, and thus a 53-card deck.

California prayer book: CALIFORNIA BIBLE.

call: Match a bet on the current round of betting and stay in competition for the pot, as opposed to FOLD or RAISE. Also CALL A BET or SEE A BET.

call a bet: CALL.

call a bluff: Call the bet of an opponent suspected of betting or raising with inferior cards.

call a player down: Match an opponent's bets (not raise) to the last round.

call a raise cold: Match a bet and a raise without having yet put any bets into the pot during the round.

call cold: Match a bet and one or more raises (two or more bets in a limit game and the equivalent in a no-limit game) without yet having put in any bets in a round. Also, *cold call.*

calling hand: A hand that is good enough to call with, but not raise.

calling station: Unflattering term for a player who calls too many bets and rarely raises.

can't buy a hand: 1. An expression that indicates luck so bad that a player couldn't get good cards even if he were allowed to buy them in a game. **2.** An expression that describes a player whose bluff bets consistently get called, thus rendering him unable to buy the pot.

can't stand a raise: A hand that isn't strong enough to call additional bets and would be folded if an opponent raised.

canine: In hold'em, hole cards of K-9.

can't get away from a hand: Being committed to and playing a strong hand to the end even in a situation in which it appears to be a loser.

cap: 1. A ceiling on the number of raises permitted in a round. For example, in limit games, many cardrooms permit a maximum of one bet and three raises. **2.** Put in the last raise permissible in a round.

capped: When the maximum number of raises has been reached in a betting round and no more are permitted.

"Cappuccino": Modification of the word "cap" to indicate that the limit for raises in the round has been reached.

card dead: Condition of being dealt one bad hand after another; essentially getting no good cards to play.

card player: One who plays card or poker games.

Card Player: A magazine devoted to poker.

cardroom: 1. A legally licensed poker facility. **2.** A place that hosts poker games. **3.** The venue or actual room in which games of poker are played.

cards: 1. The standard deck of 52 flat rectangular objects, usually made of paper, plastic, or paper coated with plastic, consisting of 13 ranks, ace through king in each of four suits (hearts, clubs, diamonds, spades), that are used to play poker, as well as many other card games. Also *deck of cards*, *pack of cards*. **2.** Specifically *good* cards. "I've been getting cards all night." "I haven't seen any cards in the last hour."

"cards in the air": Announcement that the cards are being dealt. "Ladies and gentlemen, the cards will be in the air in five minutes."

card sense: Natural ability to play skillful card or poker games.

card shark: 1. A skillful manipulator of cards, that is, a card cheat. **2.** An expert card player, usually a professional gambler. This usage of the term is not necessarily synonymous with *cheater*.

cardsharp: Any cheating player, usually implying one who manipulates the cards.

cards speak: 1. A rule stating that the value of a hand is the final arbiter in a showdown, not a player's call or miscall of it. **2.** In HIGH-LOW variants generally seen only in private games, the stipulation that high or low hands are won by the value of their rankings at the showdown, as opposed to DECLARATION, in which a player is eligible to win only the part of the pot that he announces.

cards that work together: 1. In hold'em and Omaha, cards that form good straight and flush possibilities. **2.** In Omaha, cards that coordinate well to make straights, flushes, or good high-low combinations.

case: The very last one of its type. For example, the *case ace* would be the last remaining ace in the deck. "When Joe bet his case chips and lost, we didn't see him again."

case ace: The last remaining ace.

case chips: A player's last chips.

cash: 1. Real currency issued by a government, as opposed to CHIPS, which are issued by a casino and used to replace cash in gambling games. **2.** Be among the top finishers in a tournament and win a cash prize. **3.** Win money. **4.** Change chips into money. Also, *cash in*.

cash game: 1. A game played for real money. **2.** A non-tournament game. "At the end of the tournament, the players all jumped into cash games."

cashier's cage: CAGE.

cash in: Take chips to the CAGE and exchange them for money; often implies leaving a game.

cash plays: An indication that betting cash is permissible in a game typically using chips (as is typical in all cardrooms) as the main betting currency. You may see a sign in a poker room stating, "Cash plays, $100 bills only."

casino: An establishment that hosts gambling games.

casino poker: 1. Poker played in casinos. **2.** The style or rules used in such games.

catch: Get a card that improves one's hand.

catch a piece of the flop: When some portion of a player's hole cards combine with the flop, improving his hand or providing a draw.

catch bad: Get a card that doesn't help a hand or actually hurts it.

catch good: Get a card that is beneficial to a hand.

catch perfect: 1. In lowball, draw a card that is the best possible card to improve a hand. For example, if you draw a 4 to 7-3-2-A, you *catch perfect*. **2.** In lowball, draw a perfect low, that is, a WHEEL. **3.** In hold'em, catch one of only a few possible cards that turn a losing hand into a winner.

catch up: Improve an inferior hand enough so that it is closer in strength to a hand believed to be superior.

caught in the middle: A player caught between two aggressive bettors. One so caught might be termed a *squeezed player* or said to be *whipsawed*.

center pot: MAIN POT, as opposed to a SIDE POT.

chance: 1. The possibility that an event will occur. **2.** A lucky occurrence.

change color: Change high denomination chips to lower denominations or vice versa.

change gears: Alter one's playing style during a game from, for example, loose to tight, tight to loose, conservative to aggressive, or aggressive to conservative. Also *switch gears*.

change-in: BUY-IN (both definitions).

chase: To unwisely call bets or raises on hands that are behind.

chat: Conversational interchange, in the form of typed text, in an online cardroom.

cheaply: Being able to continue playing for no bets or just a small bet.

cheat: 1. Play outside the prescribed or accepted rules of a game to gain an unfair and illegal advantage over opponents. **2.** A player who cheats. Also, *thief*.

check: 1. The act of "not betting" and passing the bet option to the next player while still remaining an active player. Once a bet has been made in a round, checking is not an option. **2.** CHIP.

check and raise: CHECK-RAISE.

check-call: Check and then call if an opponent bets, as opposed to CHECK-RAISE or CHECK-FOLD.

check-check: Check after an opponent has checked.

check-fold: Check and then fold if an opponent bets.

check in the dark: Check blindly, that is, without looking at the latest card or cards dealt.

check it down: 1. Check on the last round of betting. **2.** In a tournament, what two players implicitly agree to do when a third player is all in before the final card, that is, not make any further bets, since the all-in player is more likely to bust out against two players, thus increasing the chances for both of them to advance.

check-raise: 1. Raise in a round after first checking, essentially trapping a player. Also, *sandbag*. **2.** The strategy of checking to induce an opponent into betting so that the bet can be raised.

checks: Casino CHIPS.

Chinese poker: A card game using poker rankings, played with four players each getting thirteen cards that are formed into three hands of, respectively, three, five, and five cards, each of which competes against the hands of the other players.

chip: A token, typically round and made of clay or plastic, and of various colors and denominations, that is used as a form of currency in gambling games. Also, *check*.

chip (chipping) away: Bet small amounts with a superior hand, looking to get called—but not so much that an opponent will fold—so that the opponent's stack is steadily reduced.

chip burner: 1. A hand likely to lose large amounts of chips if played. **2.** One who plays recklessly.

chip chatter: Gossip that occurs around a poker table or among poker players.

chip count: 1. The number of chips a player has. **2.** A request to have a player's chips counted. **3.** The act of counting those chips.

chip leader: In a tournament, the player with the most chips.

chip runner: A casino or cardroom employee who sells chips to seated players.

chop: 1. Split the pot equally with one or more opponents as a result of a tie between winning hands. **2.** In a BLIND game, agree that if it comes down to just the small and big blind, each will take back the blind and not play out the hand. Also, *split the blinds*.

chump: 1. Sucker. **2.** Terrible poker player. **3.** MARK.

clean: 1. An honest dealer, player, or game. **2.** A dealer who deals an efficient game.

clean out: Win all or virtually all of the money from a player or a game.

clip joint: Cardroom or game in which players are dealt dishonest games or get cheated.

"Clock": A call by a player to have a floorperson give a slow opponent sixty seconds (or some other preestablished time constraint) to make a play or have his hand automatically folded.

closed card: A card that is FACE DOWN and can be viewed only by the player holding the card, or, if a community card, one that cannot yet be viewed by any player.

closed game: 1. A game in which all the player's cards are dealt face down. **2.** A game in which no outsiders are allowed to play.

closed poker: Any form of poker in which all players cards are dealt face down.

clubs: One of the four suits in a deck of CARDS, using a black club symbol (♣), consisting of 13 cards, 2-3-4-5-6-7-8-9-10-J-Q-K-A.

C-note: $100 or a $100 bill.

coin flip: COIN TOSS.

coin toss: A hand or situation whose winning chances approximate 50-50, that is, one in which neither side has a great advantage over the other. For example, in hold'em, A-K versus two queens is a coin-toss situation.

cojones: **1.** The NUTS (from Spanish). **2.** What a fearless player is said to possess.

cold: **1.** A player who is barely winning any pots. **2.** Little or no betting on a hand. **3.** A raise and a bet both of which need to be called by a player in a round, when part of, for example, the phrase *call a raise cold*.

cold call: CALL COLD.

cold steal: Betting a weak hand aggressively to force opponents to fold, that is, a BLUFF.

collection: TIME COLLECTION.

color: Change chips to ones of higher or lower denominations.

color change: **1.** See CHANGE COLOR. **2.** An announcement by a house dealer or floor person that a player is changing color.

color down: Change chips to ones of lower denominations.

color up: Change chips to ones of higher denominations.

come back at: Raise a bettor or raiser. "On the flop, he led at me, and I came right back at him without hesitation."

come down: Draw a particular hand. "When the 7 appeared on the turn, he came down with a set of sevens."

come hand: A hand that needs at least one more card to improve to a ranking of sufficient value to win, usually a straight or flush draw that needs a fifth card to complete.

come in cold: Enter the pot having to call a bet and at least one raise without having placed any chips into the pot during the betting round. See CALL COLD.

come in for: Enter a pot as the first bettor; followed by an amount or equivalent, for example, *come in for $100* or *come in for a raise*. Also, *bring it in*.

come in for a raise: Enter the pot by raising the BLIND, that is, in a limit game, by putting in twice the size of the BIG BLIND and in a no-limit game by raising at least the size of the big blind.

come off: A card that gets dealt, as in *a deuce came off on the turn*.

come over the top: 1. Raise or reraise. "When Billy raised my bet on the turn, I came over the top for all my chips." **2.** In no-limit and pot-limit games, make specifically a large raise or reraise.

coming in: Betting first in a round, for example, *he raised coming in on the flop*.

commit: Put chips into a pot so that another card can be seen (not to be confused with POT-COMMITTED).

community cards: In hold'em and Omaha, the cards dealt to the center of the table that are shared by all players. Also, *board*.

community pot: FAMILY POT.

complete: Improve a three- or four-card drawing hand to a straight or flush, or improve a two-pair hand to a full house; also, *fill*.

completed: 1. A bet being brought up to its nominal level after a minimal bring-in. For example, in a $5/$10 seven-card stud game, the low card might be forced to make a $2 bring-in. Anyone acting thereafter can either call the $2 or complete to $5. **2.** A SHORT BET being brought to its proper size on a subsequent bet.

completed bet: 1. A bet that was made with too few chips for the required amount having been brought up to the proper size. For example, $100 is bet and a player calls $95. When he puts that missing $5 into the pot, that is a *completed bet*. **2.** A player's all-in bet being below the minimum level, and a subsequent player putting out more chips to meet the proper size. Also see FULL BET. For example, in a $10/$20 game, an all-in player puts in his last $15, the next player can *make it a completed bet* by making it $20, with that extra $5 going into a side pot among remaining players who call the $20 bet.

complete hand: 1. In high poker, usually a five-card straight or flush, as opposed to a DRAWING HAND. **2.** In low poker, usually an 8 or better. For both definitions, also MADE HAND.

complete the bet: An action to bring a bet of insufficient size up to the proper amount.

compulsive gambler: One who obsessively gambles away money to the point that it harms his personal or professional life.

concealed: 1. Cards held by a player and seen only by him. Also, *closed cards, downcards.* **2.** Cards whose strength is hidden or a hand played in such a way that opponents are misled into thinking that the player has a hand of much lesser value. For example, in seven-card stud, a player with a board of four apparently unrelated and otherwise innocuous cards can have a concealed straight or full house. Often part of the phrase *concealed hand.*

concealed hand: See CONCEALED.

connecting cards: Cards in consecutive or near-consecutive order such that a straight can be formed, for example, 7-8-9 or 7-8-10.

connectors: Two or more cards in sequence, such as 5-6 or J-Q.

consecutive declaration: In HIGH-LOW games, when players *declare* (announce) in turn which part of the pot they are playing for (high, low, or high and low) and can win only what they declare, as opposed to CARDS SPEAK. (*Consecutive declaration* is not played in public games in cardrooms and casinos, where *cards speak* is the standard.) Compare to SIMULTANEOUS DECLARATION.

coordinated board: A board with flush or straight draws.

coordinated cards: Cards that work well together and can form many combinations, used in Omaha when referring to the four hole cards.

coordinated flop: In hold'em and Omaha, a flop with good straight and flush draws, such as 9-10-J or 7-5-4 of mixed suits, or cards with two or three matching suits.

correct odds: The exact mathematical odds of an event occurring or not occurring. For example, the correct odds against pulling the green chip out of a bag containing one green chip and two red ones are 2 to 1 against.

correct play: Either the mathematically best play or the best play given the circumstances.

counterfeited: When a key card in a player's hand is duplicated by another of the same rank being dealt, rendering that card useless to the player. For example, if a player going for low has 2-3-4-7 and receives a 2, his deuce has been *counterfeited*. Also, *duplicated*.

"Count it down": A request for a player or dealer to count a chip stack and verify the exact amount held or being bet.

court card: FACE CARD.

covered: Have equal to or more than enough chips to meet a bet, usually an all-in bet. For example, on an all-in call, if the winner has $17,000 and the loser less than $17,000, the winner is said to have the loser covered.

cowboys: Kings.

crabs: In hold'em, hole cards of 3-3.

cracked: A strong starting hand that gets busted by a stronger one. In hold'em, often refers to aces. "He cracked my pocket aces when he flopped a set."

◆───────

crazy pineapple: A variation of PINEAPPLE in which players discard one of their three hole cards *after* the flop.

cripple: **1.** Hold cards that opponents need or for needed open cards to already be in play, or discarded and unavailable. **2.** In a tournament, administer such a bad loss that an opponent's bankroll is severely depleted, putting his tournament survival in dire jeopardy. "Losing with those kings crippled him and he had to go all in on the next hand."

crippled deck: When most or all of the cards needed to improve a hand are already in play and thus unavailable, for example, a deck is *crippled* for a player holding two kings in seven-card stud when he sees two other kings out on the board.

crossfire: Getting caught between a bettor and one or more raisers. Usually part of the phrase *caught in the crossfire*. This is also called being *whipsawed*.

crossroader: Professional cheat.

crying call: 1. A reluctant call with a weak or speculative hand, hoping that it doesn't get raised so that another card can be seen without added cost. **2.** A call made on the end knowing that one is likely beat.

curve: In a tournament, the average stack size. For example, with 10 players and $100,000 in chips, the curve is $10,000 and players with more chips would be *above the curve*, and those with fewer chips would be *below the curve*.

customer: 1. Someone calling a bet in a situation likely favorable for the bettor. "Ah, I've got a customer." **2.** Disparaging term for a weak player who contributes money to more skilled players at the table. Also, PRODUCER.

cut: 1. The money taken out of the pot by the house as its fee for running the game. Also *house cut, vigorish, rake*. **2.** Separating the cards into two or more piles and restacking them in a different order, an act usually performed by a house dealer in a cardroom after shuffling the cards, and by the player to the right of the dealer in a private game. **3.** A percentage of profits taken by an investor or partner.

cut card: A card that is not part of the deck (and typically of a different and distinct color) that is used to separate the deck into two stacks so that the top and bottom order of the packs can be reversed for the safety of the players against cheating, as well as for the purpose of covering the bottom card of the deck for protection against accidental exposure. Also, *security card*.

cutoff: CUTOFF SEAT.

cutoff seat: The position to the right of the BUTTON.

cut the cards: Divide a deck of cards into two or more piles for the purpose of having them restacked in a different order, a standard procedure in card games to help protect players against nonrandom shuffles.

d: Symbol for diamonds in written text. 8d is the 8♦.

dance: Bet and actively pursue the pot. A player might throw a bet into the pot and say, "Anyone want to dance with me?"

dangler: In Omaha, a fourth starting card that doesn't match well or work with the others in the group. For example, with starting cards of J-Q-K-4, the 4 is a *dangler* to the three high cards; in the hand 2-3-4-K, the king is a dangler.

dark: See BET IN THE DARK.

day shift: Morning shift. Also *a.m.*

dead: 1. A hand that has no chance of winning no matter what card is drawn; usually as part of the phrase DRAWING DEAD. **2.** A card that is declared out of play due to some irregularity or one that has already been played and therefore cannot get drawn. **3.** A game that has little action or is boring, often as part of the phrase *dead game* or *dead spread*. **4.** A hand that is ruled invalid and out of contention for the pot because the player has been given a time limit to make a play and did not do so within the required time frame, because one or more of its cards fell on the floor, or because of some other infraction of the rules.

dead blind: 1. A blind position that cannot raise the pot unless it is already raised. Compare to LIVE BLIND, typical in hold'em and Omaha, in which the little or big blind can raise the pot. **2.** Blind bet that is surrendered to the next pot and cannot be won because all players have folded. Compare to typical hold'em games in which the pot is won by the big blind by default if no one opens.

dead broke: Completely without money. Also, *flat broke.*

dead card: 1. A card that has been deemed invalid and out of play due to an irregularity. **2.** A card that has already been played and therefore cannot get drawn.

dead game: See DEAD.

dead hand: 1. A hand ruled invalid because of a misdeal or where cards have been inadvertently or accidentally exposed by the dealer. **2.** A hand that is ruled dead and out of contention for the pot because the player has been given a time limit to make a play and did not do so within the required time frame.

dead man's hand: Aces and eights, the hand held by "Wild Bill" Hickok in 1876 when he was shot dead in a poker game in Deadwood, South Dakota. The fifth card in the hand is not known.

dead money: 1. Disparaging term for a player who has little chance of winning. **2.** Money put into the pot by players who have folded and are no longer in competition for it.

dead spread: See DEAD.

deadwood: A player who is easy pickings for better players.

deal: 1. The act of distributing cards to the players. **2.** The dealer's position. A player might ask, "Where is the deal?"
3. In a tournament, an agreement between players at a final table to divide a certain portion of the prize money before the final outcome as a way of reducing the risk of losing the first place money and increasing the bottom line win of the remaining players. "Skinny Tommy, The Suit, and Chuckles made a deal when they got three-handed." Also, *save.*
4. Distribute cards. "Deal me in."

POKER TALK

dealer: The person who shuffles the cards and deals them out to all the players. In a private game, the dealer is usually a player as well. In a public game, the dealer is usually a house employee and not a participant in the game and has the additional responsibility of running the game smoothly.

dealer button: See BUTTON.

dealer position: DEAL, definition 2.

dealer's choice: Poker in which the choice of games rotates around the table and the person whose turn it is to deal gets to choose the variation played.

deal in: Distribute cards to, and include a player in, a hand. Also *shuffle in*.

"Deal me in": Instruction given to the dealer that a player wants to be dealt cards.

"Deal me out": 1. An instruction given to the dealer by a player to skip his turn of play. **2.** A declaration that a player is going to quit play altogether.

deal out: Skip a player's turn on a hand, either temporarily or on a more permanent basis. "Deal me out; I'm taking a break."

deception: Checking, betting, or raising in a manner that has the purpose of fooling opponents into thinking a hand of a different strength is held.

deck: 1. The pack of cards used for play. **2.** In standard, non-wild versions of poker, the pack of 52 cards, made up of 13 cards, ace through king in each of four suits (hearts, clubs, diamonds, spades), that are used to play poker as well as any number of card games. Also, see CARDS. Also *deck of cards*, *pack of cards*.

deck of cards: See DECK.

declaration: 1. Announcement of one's hand, usually at the showdown. **2.** In HIGH-LOW games in which players *declare* (announce) either in turn (CONSECUTIVE DECLARATION) or simultaneously which part of the pot they are playing for (high, low, or high and low) and can win only what they declare, as opposed to CARDS SPEAK.

deep: The number of chips a player has, particularly in no-limit games, and often part of the phrase "How DEEP ARE YOU?"

defend a hand: Call a bet or raise with a hand believed to be of sufficient value to justify the added cost of playing.

defend the blind: In the small or big blind position, call a raise made by an opponent in middle to late position who is suspected of raising to force out opponents so that he can STEAL THE BLINDS.

defensive bet: 1. A bet, usually a small one, in a no-limit game to discourage a larger bet by an opponent. **2.** A bet made in any poker variation to discourage further action in the current or following rounds.

denomination: The value or rank of a card, for example, a 2 or a jack. (Denomination does not refer to the suit.) Also, *rank*.

deuce: 1. The 2 in any suit. In high poker, the lowest card value; in ace-five low poker, the second lowest and best card after the ace; in deuce-seven, the best low card. **2.** A $2-limit game. "Do you have a seat in the deuce?" **3.** A bet of $2, $200, or $2,000, the amount being understood in the context of the limit played.

deuces wild: Poker in which the four deuces act as wild cards, and can be used as any rank and suit, including as a duplicate of a card already held by another player. For example, A♠ J♠ 9♠ 8♠ 3♠, would lose to 2♥ Q♠ 7♠ 5♠ 3♠ because the 2♥ would serve as an A♠ (even though the other player holds an A♠) making the A-Q flush higher than the A-J flush.

deuce-to-seven: Low poker in which the lowest and best card is a deuce and the highest, and therefore worst, is an ace. Flushes and straights count against the player, so the best hand is 2-3-4-5-7 of mixed suits. Also called *deuce-to-seven lowball, Kansas City lowball.* Compare with ACE-TO-FIVE.

deuce-to-seven lowball: DEUCE-TO-SEVEN.

diamonds: One of the four suits in a deck of cards, using a red diamond symbol (♦), consisting of 13 cards, 2-3-4-5-6-7-8-9-10-J-Q-K-A.

die with a hand: Be committed to or play a big hand to the river and lose.

dime: Literally, 10¢, but in the context of a poker game not played for small change, commonly used to indicate a $10, $1,000, or a $10,000 chip or bet, depending on the size of the game and the context.

direction: In a HIGH-LOW game, the part of a pot that a player is trying to win—high, low, or high-low.

discard: In draw poker, get rid of a card or cards so that new ones may be drawn.

discard pile: The area on a table where cards taken out of play are put. Also *muck* or *muck pile*.

discards: Cards that are folded, burned, or are no longer in play.

disproportionate bet: In no-limit or pot-limit, a bet larger than is customary or a situation warrants.

doctored cards: Cards that have been altered by a cheat.

dog: A hand or situation that is unlikely to win, and is not the favorite; short for UNDERDOG.

dollar: 1. $1 or a $1 chip or bet in small games. **2.** In larger games, $100 or a $100 chip or bet.

Dolly Parton: In hold'em, hole cards of 9-5; named after the movie in which the actress starred.

dominated hand: A hand that is greatly inferior to another such that it will lose a great majority of times. For example, K-9 is a *dominated hand* against A-K.

dominating: A starting hand vastly superior to another such that it will win most confrontations. For example, K-Q dominates Q-J and A-A dominates K-K. Often used to indicate a hand, such as in the former example, in which one card is duplicated and the other is higher.

door card: In stud variations, the first open card dealt to each player.

double add-on tournament: An ADD-ON TOURNAMENT that allows players a final purchase of two additional specified allotments of chips, usually at the end of the first few rounds of play.

double ante: When the antes in an unopened pot are applied to the next deal along with a new ante such that each player has anted twice.

double belly buster: A non-OPEN-ENDED STRAIGHT draw with two GAPS such that a straight can be filled by two ranks, providing the same number of outs (eight) as an open-ended straight. For example, in hold'em, with hole cards of 9-7 and a board of J-5-8, any 6 or 10 will make a straight. Also, *double gutshot*.

double bet: 1. A bet and raise that is owed or made. **2.** Two bets, as opposed to a single bet, where only one bet is owed or made. This is usually in a limit game and often part of a dealer's announcement. "It's a double bet to you" (or triple or quadruple bet). **3.** In seven-card stud, a bet on fourth street that is double the normal size for the round and can be made if an open pair is showing anywhere. **4.** BIG BET.

double-bet level: In limit poker with a two-tier structure, the second and higher level of betting that occurs in the latter rounds, as opposed to *single-bet level*. For example, in a $5/$10 game, the $10 level of betting. Also *two bet level*.

double bluff: 1. A bluff bet made by betting or raising an opponent with inferior cards, then reraising an opponent's raise. **2.** A bluff bet made on consecutive betting rounds.

double-ended straight: Four consecutive cards to a straight such as 2-3-4-5, in which a card on either end will make a straight, as opposed to an *inside, gutshot,* or *one-way straight.* Also, *eight-way straight, open-ended straight, open-ended draw.* (A double-ended straight cannot include an ace.)

double-gapper: A nonconsecutive straight draw with two gaps, such as 2-4-5-6-8 (which is possible only in poker games in which players can make hands with more than five cards, such as seven-card stud and flop games), in which one of two cards can be drawn to form a straight; as, a 4 or a 7 in this example. Also, DOUBLE BELLY BUSTER and *two-gapper.*

double gutshot: DOUBLE BELLY BUSTER.

double limit: The two-tier structure of LIMIT games, such as $3/$6, $30/$60, and $40/$80, in which the lower limit is the required bet or raise in the early betting rounds, and the higher limit is the required bet or raise for the latter betting rounds. Compare to SINGLE LIMIT, POT LIMIT, and NO LIMIT.

double raise: A raise and a reraise in a round.

double-suited: A hand that has possibilities of making a flush in either of two suits; usually refers to a starting Omaha hand with two cards each of two suits.

double through: 1. Double one's bankroll on a single hand, by being all-in against another player and winning the showdown. Also, *run through, double up.* **2** Double one's bankroll in a session.

double up: See DOUBLE THROUGH.

down: 1. A card dealt face down so that its value is known only to the holder of the card. **2.** Losing money. "He was down $1,100 after those two hands."

down and out: Being in distressing circumstances, usually without money and in low spirits.

"Down and dirty": In a stud game, an announcement of the last card (which is dealt face down).

downcard: A card that can be viewed only by the player holding it; HOLE CARD. Any card that is not exposed to players. Opposite of UPCARD.

down to the felt: 1. Low-stacked and nearly out of chips. "After the bad beat with his aces, he was down to the felt." **2.** Broke; having no money left.

Doyle Brunson: 1. The legendary player and author of *Super System*, the bible of poker. **2.** In hold'em, hole cards of 10-2, the hand that Doyle Brunson won the championship with in 1976 and 1977.

drag the pot: Pull in the chips from the pot after a win.

draw: 1. In DRAW POKER variations, the exchange of unwanted cards for fresh ones. **2.** The point in draw poker at which the draw occurs. **3.** Short name for the game of draw poker. **4.** In a tournament, a random selection assigning tables and seat numbers to players or the player's assignment thus received.

draw dead: Have a hand with more cards to come that is hopelessly beat, no matter what cards are dealt. "Joe picked up a 9 to complete his 10-J-Q-K straight draw, but was drawing dead to a player already holding a flush."

drawing hand: A hand that needs improvement to form some strength, usually referring to an unmade straight or flush.

draw live: Drawing to a hand that has chances of winning, as opposed to DRAW DEAD.

draw lowball: LOWBALL.

draw out: 1. The improvement of an inferior hand into a good one by the drawing of advantageous cards. **2.** Improve an inferior hand with a good draw such that it beats an opponent who previously had a stronger hand, often referring to a three- or four-card straight or flush that fills. When used in reference to a hand that is not currently the best beating a better hand, *draw out on.* A stronger rendering of this term is SUCK OUT or SUCK OUT ON.

draw out on: DRAW OUT.

draw poker: 1. Form of poker in which each player receives (usually five) cards face down, there is a betting round, each player can exchange unwanted cards for fresh ones (the DRAW), followed by a second betting round, and then the showdown. **2.** Specifically high draw poker. Often called *five-card draw*.

draw to: Attempt to improve to a better hand. "He was drawing to a flush for all his chips."

draw to the nuts: Have a straight, flush, or straight flush draw, that, if filled, will give the player the best possible hand of its type. For example, a player holding A♠ J♠ in hold'em would be *drawing to the nuts* on a flop of K♠ 9♦ 2♠.

drop: 1. Fold. **2.** Lose money. **3.** RAKE.

drop-in: A player who comes unexpectedly to a poker game.

dry: 1. A pot or game with little or no money to be won. **2.** Out of money.

dry pot: A bet made into a SIDE POT that currently contains nothing; usually heard as part of the phrase *bet into a dry pot*. **2.** A pot with very little money in it to be won.

dump: Fold a hand.

duplicated: COUNTERFEITED.

early action button: In online poker, an option to select a play before it is one's turn to act. Also, *preselect button*.

early out: 1. To bust out of a tournament during the first few rounds. **2.** In a cardroom, a dealer who leaves the shift early.

early position: Approximately the first third of players to act in a nine- or 10-handed game or the first or second to act in a six- or seven-handed game.

earn respect: Play in a manner such that when bets or raises are made, opponents give one credit for holding a strong hand as opposed to a weak hand held by a bluffer.

easy money: 1. Profit made without much effort or risk. **2.** When a player enjoys a large, almost unfair advantage over opponents.

edge: Having a winning expectation. Also, *advantage*.

effective odds: IMPLIED ODDS.

8: The card with eight pips on it and the number 8. A standard deck has four such cards, one in each suit.

eight-handed: 1. A poker game played with eight players or a game that currently has eight players seated. **2.** A pot contested by eight players.

8-nothing: In lowball or high-low, 8-4-3-2-A.

8-perfect: 8-NOTHING.

eight-way straight: OPEN-ENDED STRAIGHT, having eight OUTS to fill, such as 4-5-6-7, needing either a 3 or an 8 to complete. Also *open-ended straight, double-ended straight, open-ended draw*.

8-or-better: In HIGH-LOW POKER, a requirement that a player must have a card no higher than an 8 and no cards paired for his five-card hand to QUALIFY for the low end of the pot. If no player has such a hand, the highest hand at the showdown wins the entire pot. See QUALIFIER.

eights: A pair of eights.

eighty-sixed: 1. Barred from play. **2.** Being kicked out.

eleven-handed: 1. A poker game played with eleven players or a game that currently has eleven players seated. **2.** A pot contested by eleven players.

"El Paso": "To fold."

eliminated: In a tournament, when a player has lost all his chips and is knocked out of play.

emergency low: In a high-low game, a hand being played primarily to win the high half of the pot but that also has low potential, albeit not a very good low on its own. For example, the A-8 combination would be considered an *emergency low* in the Omaha starting hand of A-A-K-8.

encourage action: Bet, hoping other players will call or raise, putting more bets into the pot.

end: The last card or cards dealt; often part of the phrase *on the end*. Also, in seven-card stud and flop games, *river*.

enter the pot: Get involved in a pot by betting or calling.

entry fee: The cost to participate in a tournament, usually collected by a cardroom or casino in addition to the BUY-IN. For example, in a $1,000 + $30 tournament, the buy-in is $1,000 and the entry fee is $30.

equity: 1. The amount of money invested in a hand or in a game. **2.** The amount of money in a pot a player would expect to win if the hand were played out over the long run, for example, if the player had a one-third chance of winning a $120 pot, his *equity* would be $40. Sometimes the entire cost of a tournament including buy-in and tournaments fees.

escape cards: OUTS, that is, cards that will make a hand a winner.

etiquette: Established and accepted rules of proper behavior in a poker game.

EV: EXPECTED VALUE.

even: 1. Neither winning nor losing, having exactly or close to the same amount of chips or funds as when one started a session or a given period of time. "I'm even for the month." **2.** Having an equal or about equal chance of winning or losing. "I had an even shot at the pot."

even money: 1. A bet in which either side has about an equal chance of winning. **2.** A bet that pays $1 for every $1 wagered.

expectation: The expected profit or loss given the mathematical likelihood of winning a situation. Expectation is usually expressed as being positive or negative, or given as a dollar amount. "This play has positive expectation." "In this situation, my expectation is $23 for every $100 bet."

expected value: The amount of money likely to be won (or lost) over a specified period of time given the odds of the situation. Often called *EV*, and it can be positive or negative.

expensive: 1. Having to face relatively high betting to enter or continue playing in a pot or a game. **2.** A large loss.

expert player: A seasoned player with superior skills and a winning EXPECTATION against most opponents.

exposed card: A dealt or undealt card, or a downcard that is inadvertently revealed to players.

extra bet: A bet or raise that forces a player to call one more bet to continue on in a hand.

eyes of Texas: Pair of aces.

face: 1. The side of a card that indicates its value. **2.** FACE CARD.

face card: Any jack, queen, or king. Also *face, court card, paint, picture card.*

face down: A card positioned such that its rank and suit faces the table and cannot be viewed. A DOWNCARD, HOLE CARD, or CLOSED CARD is dealt *face down.* Opposite of FACE UP.

face-face: Unpaired cards having the rank jack, queen, or king.

face-to-face poker: REAL-WORLD POKER.

face up: A card positioned such that its rank and suit faces up and is therefore visible to all players. Cards so dealt are called *open cards.* Opposite of FACE DOWN.

fade the white line: Term coined by Texas road gamblers who figuratively followed the white line on the highway as they traveled from place to place to find poker games.

fall: Be dealt, as a card. "A jack fell on the turn."

false openers: A bet with a hand that is not legally strong enough to open the betting (that is, does not contain OPENERS), usually associated with JACKS OR BETTER draw poker.

family pot: A hand in which all or almost all of the players are involved. Also *community pot*.

fancy play: Checking, betting, or raising in a situation that goes against conventional wisdom, with the purpose of deceiving opponents.

fast: 1. A game with lots of action. **2.** A player who aggressively bets and raises. **3.** A game played at a rapid pace.

fast action tournament: A tournament with levels of twenty minutes or less.

fast company: Players who don't play an honest game.

fast game: A poker game with a lot of betting.

fatten the pot: Put more bets into a pot.

favorite: 1. A hand or situation that is likely to win or perceived to be likely to win; as opposed to UNDERDOG. **2.** An event that is mathematically likely to occur. **3.** A bet that pays less per unit in winnings than is risked. For example, when betting a 3 to 2 favorite, one bets $2 to win $3. **4.** A situation that is more likely to occur than any other situation, even though overall, it may be likely not to occur. For example, in hold'em, with seven hands played to the river, pocket aces are the favorite to win compared to any other individual hand, although the aces are an overall underdog against the field.

fearless: Having no fear of making bets or raises in any situation, regardless of risk.

feed the pot: Put more bets into a pot, usually unwisely.

feeler bet: Small bet or raise designed to see how opponents will react, and thus get information on the quality of their hands.

feeler raise: Raise designed to see how an opponent will react and reveal the quality of his hand.

field: The group of active players in a hand or a tournament or the total number of players. For example, a player who bets first with seven players behind him is said to have *bet into the field*. A tournament with 2,576 entrants is said to have a *field* of 2,576.

fifth street: 1. In seven-card stud, the fifth card dealt to players along with the betting round accompanying it. **2.** In hold'em and Omaha, the final round of betting, named for the fifth COMMUNITY CARD dealt; more commonly called the RIVER.

53rd card: The JOKER.

53-card deck: A standard 52-card DECK plus one JOKER.

52-card deck: The standard DECK of cards used in poker, containing ace through king in four suits for a total of 52 cards.

fill: 1. Draw a card to complete a five-card hand such as a straight, flush, or full house. "Mac's jacks and fives filled when a jack fell on the river." **2.** Replenish the chip bank, a term used by dealers.

fill up: Make a FULL HOUSE.

final table: In a tournament, the final table of players, which comes with prestige, especially in major tournaments, and typically includes cash prizes.

fire a bet: Bet or raise, particularly in a confident fashion.

first player in the pot: In a betting round, the first player to make a bet.

first position: The first player to ACT, particularly in the first round. The player in first position is UNDER THE GUN.

first to act: The player who goes first in a betting round.

fish: 1. Weak player. Also *customer, live one, pigeon, provider*.
2. Call bets or raises with a weak hand in the hopes of making a longshot draw. Often *fish in*.

fish in: See FISH.

fishing: Calling bets or raises with a weak hand hoping to make a longshot draw. Often *fishing in*.

5: The card with five pips on it and the number 5. A standard deck has four such cards, one in each suit.

five: Fifth street.

five-card draw: 1. A poker variation featuring five closed cards per player, two betting rounds, and a chance to exchange unwanted cards for new ones—called the draw. Usually played as high poker. Also called *draw poker*. **2.** In draw poker variations, the exchanging of five unwanted cards on the draw for five new ones. "There were three one-card draws and a five-card draw."

five-card stud: A poker variation in which each player starts with one face-up and one face-down card, there is a betting round, and then each player receives three successive face-up cards one at a time, each followed by a betting round, for a total of four betting rounds.

five-handed: 1. A poker game played with five players or a game that currently has five players seated. **2.** A pot contested by five players.

five of a kind: A hand with five cards of the same rank, such as five sixes, which is possibly only in wild-card games.

fiver: A $5 bet or a 5 in any suit.

fives: A pair of fives.

five-way: A pot contested by five players.

fixed limit: A form of betting in which limits are predetermined in advance, usually in a two-tier structure (often called DOUBLE LIMIT) such as $5/$10, $10/$20, or $40/$80, with the first, lower amount being used for the early rounds of betting, and the latter, higher amount used for later rounds. Compare with POT-LIMIT and NO-LIMIT. Also called STRUCTURED LIMIT.

flag: A high-denomination poker chip, usually $5,000.

flash: 1. Inadvertently or purposely expose closed cards, dealt or undealt. **2.** Purposely expose a card or cards to a confederate as parting of a cheating scam.

flat bet: Bet the same amount (as previously).

flat broke: DEAD BROKE.

flat call: SMOOTH CALL.

flat limit: Single limit.

flight: Any of the two or more starting dates for a tournament when the host casino cannot accommodate all the players on a single starting date. For example, the 2005 World Series of Poker had three first-day *flights* of approximately 1,800-2,000 players each so that Rio Hotel and Casino could accommodate the massive field of 5,619 players.

floor: 1. When announced, a call to attract a supervisor when there is a decision needed on a controversial, contentious, or unclear situation. For example, if a card left the table, the dealer might yell "Floor!" to get an official ruling on how to proceed. **2.** The physical location where poker is being played and the area immediately around that location. **3.** A supervisor on active duty. "The dealer yelled out, 'Who's on the floor?'"

floorperson: A supervisor whose responsibility is to ensure the smooth running of the games, including settling disputes and managing dealers. Often shortened to *floor*.

flop: In hold'em and Omaha, the three COMMUNITY CARDS that are simultaneously dealt face up upon completion of the first round of betting and can be used by all active players.

flop bad: Get a FLOP that weakens one's hand or appears to greatly help opponents.

flop game: Poker variation, such as hold'em or Omaha, that features a FLOP, three cards exposed at one time in the middle for all players to share.

flop good: Get a flop that greatly improves one's hand.

flopped: Pocket cards that combine with the flop to form a hand or draw, as in *Ivan flopped top pair* or *Cedric flopped a straight draw.*

flop the nuts: In hold'em and Omaha, get a flop that makes the best hand possible given the three cards on the board.

flush: A poker hand consisting of five cards of the same suit, such as Q♥ 9♥ 8♥ 5♥ 2♥, a queen-high club flush.

flush card: A card that helps make a flush.

flush draw: Four cards of one suit needing one more card of that suit to complete a flush.

fold: Get rid of one's cards, thereby becoming inactive in the current hand and ineligible to play for the pot.

fold out of turn: Fold a hand before it is one's turn to act (which is a breach of poker etiquette).

force: Bet or raise such that it compels other players to make a decision. "Sammy led out on the turn to force the action."

forced bet: A mandatory bet, such as an ANTE or BLIND, that must be made by players before the cards are dealt, or in certain situations, such as the first round in seven-card stud, because a player has received the highest or lowest open card dealt—see BRING-IN, definition 1.

forced blind: BLIND.

foul: Cause a hand to become unplayable due to one of the conditions described under FOUL HAND.

foul hand: A hand that has received the wrong number of cards, was dealt out of order, or been affected by some other impropriety, and therefore is deemed illegal (that is, cannot be played).

4: The card with four pips on it and the number 4. A standard deck has four such cards, one in each suit.

four: FOURTH STREET. "John raised him on four."

four-bet: Reraise a reraiser, bringing the number of bets to four.

four bets: A call and three raises in a round. As opposed to *one bet*, in which only a single bet is owed or made. *Two bets* and *three bets* are also possible.

four-card draw: In draw poker variations, the exchanging of four unwanted cards on the draw for four new ones. "There were three one-card draws and a four-card draw."

four-card flush: A hand containing four cards of the same suit.

four-card straight: A hand containing four cards in sequence, such as 2-3-4-5, needing one more to complete the straight.

four-card straight flush: A hand containing four cards in sequence and of the same suit, such as 8♣ 9♣ 10♣ J♣.

four flush: FOUR-CARD FLUSH.

four-flusher: 1. A player who tries to win pots illegally by intentionally miscalling his hand or showing only part of a hand. **2.** A cheat.

four-straight: FOUR-CARD STRAIGHT.

four-handed: 1. A poker game played with four players or a game that currently has four players seated. **2.** A pot contested by four players.

four of a kind: A poker hand containing four cards of the same rank, such as K♣ K♠ K♥ K♦, four kings. Also, *quads*.

four-way straight: An INSIDE STRAIGHT draw, that is, four consecutive cards of mixed suits with a gap, as, 2-4-5-6, which needs any of four threes to fill.

fours: A pair of fours.

fourth street: 1. In seven-card stud, the fourth card dealt to players, along with the betting round accompanying it. **2.** In hold'em and Omaha, the third round of betting, named for the fourth COMMUNITY CARD dealt; more commonly called the TURN.

four-way: A pot contested by four players.

free card: A betting round in which all players checked, thereby allowing players to see another card without cost.

free ride: Term for a round of play where no one has made a bet—there are only checks—and thus, there is no cost to see another card.

freeroll: 1. Play a hand or a tournament, or continue playing, at no cost or risk and with only the upside of winning money. **2.** When a hand is already won and there is only potential gain and no more risk in additional betting. **3.** When a hand in an all-in bet is guaranteed at least a tie in addition to having outs for a win. For example, A♦ K♦ against A♣ K♥ with a flop of Q♠ 9♦ 7♦. Either the pot will be split or the first hand will win if a diamond comes. Here, the first hand is said to be *freerolling*. **4.** FREEROLL TOURNAMENT. **5.** Any situation where a player feels that nothing is at risk and there are only gains to be had.

freeroll tournament: 1. A tournament with no cost to enter or the buy-in has already been won through an inexpensive satellite. Often shortened to *freeroll*. **2.** A tournament that a player applies previous winnings to for his buy-in, and thus considers the event to be without cost.

freeze out: Make a large bet that opponents are unwilling to call, thus forcing them to fold.

freeze-out (tournament or game): A tournament or game played until one player has all the chips. Seen as *freeze-out tournament*, *freeze-out game*, or simply *freeze-out*.

Friday night game: Private poker game played by friends on Friday nights, although the term is often loosely applied to games played on other nights.

friendly game: Poker played casually with less emphasis on making money and more on having fun. Also, *social game*.

from behind: In LATE POSITION.

front: In EARLY POSITION. Also *front position, around front*.

front position: See FRONT.

full: 1. FULL HOUSE. **2.** The connecting term in the naming of a full house, placed after a three of a kind portion, as in *kings full*—three kings and another pair to form a full house or *kings full of deuces*.

full bet: 1. In limit games, a bet that is equal to the amount required for the round. For example, in a $10/$20 game, $10 would be a *full bet* on the first rounds, and when the limits raise, $20 would be a full bet. Compare with SHORT BET, in which a player does not have enough chips to reach that minimum level.
2. In no-limit and pot-limit games, a bet that is of the minimum amount required to open betting, or if a bet has already been made, a call or raise that is at least the size of the previous bet.

full boat: FULL HOUSE.

full buy: A buy-in to a game of at least the minimum amount required.

full deck: 1. A DECK of cards containing all fifty-two cards, as opposed to a deck that is missing cards. **2.** Crazy, when applied to an individual as part of the phrase *not playing with a full deck*.

full game: A game with a full or near-full complement of players, as opposed to a SHORTHANDED GAME.

full house: A poker hand consisting of three of a kind and a pair, such as 7-7-7-K-K, called a *full house of sevens over kings* or *sevens full of kings*, and J-J-J-3-3, a *full house of jacks over threes*. Also *full boat* or simply *full*.

full-kill game: KILL GAME.

full of: Part of the descriptive naming of a full house, with the three of a kind specified first and the pair rendered *full of*, such as A-A-A-Q-Q, which is *aces full of queens*.

full rebuy: A REBUY for more chips at the maximum amount allowed.

full table: A table of players with no empty seats.

full value: Inducing from opponents the maximum number of bets or maximum amount of money possible on a winning hand. Also see GET FULL VALUE.

gamble: 1. Put money at risk in the hopes of winning more money. **2.** Play a speculative hand for a big bet.

gambler: 1. A person who puts funds at risk in the hopes of winning money. **2.** A degenerate who consistently loses because of irresponsible gambling habits. **3.** A person who takes risks. **4.** Often, any poker player.

game: 1. A ROUND of cards dealt, ending with a showdown or an uncalled bet at any point before the showdown. **2.** A regular gathering of poker players. **3.** A type of poker variation, as hold'em or seven-card stud. **4.** Players competing against one another, generally referring to a table of players. **5.** The competitive spirit of a player; HEART. "He's got game."

game starter: SHILL. Also, *starter*.

gap: The missing card in an INSIDE STRAIGHT draw, for example, 6-7-9-10 for which an 8 is needed to make a straight.

George: Big tipper.

get an extra bet: In limit poker, induce an opponent into making an additional bet by checking into him and then raising his bet.

get a piece (of): Partially stake a player and receive a percentage of his winnings.

get a piece of the flop: In hold'em and Omaha, have one's hole cards combine with the three-card flop to form a potential winning hand, though one not necessarily favored to win.

get away cheaply: Fold a (usually) strong hand in a situation in which continuing with it would have led to a large loss of chips.

get away from a hand: Fold a strong hand against one or more hands that appear to be stronger.

get even: 1. After being down, to make a comeback so that the player has the same number of chips as when he started. **2.** The desire for this situation. "After three hours of up and down play, Skip went on a bad run and was just looking to get even."

get full value: Maximize the size of the pot by betting and raising with either the probable winning cards or a drawing hand that will win if completed. "Casey jammed the pot on every street to get full value on his set of kings."

get help: Receive a card or cards that improve a hand.

get in the last bet: Bet or raise (as opposed to checking and calling) at every opportunity so that the betting in a round stops only due to an opponent calling (and not raising) the last bet or raise. "When you have the best hand, you want to get in the last bet on every street."

get involved with: Play a pot against an opponent or several opponents.

get one's feet wet: Put a bet into the pot for the first time on a deal.

get paid off: 1. The money a player wins or stands to win. "If I make this hand, I'll get paid off." **2.** Win a pot from a player who calls a bet or raise on the end knowing he has an inferior hand but feels obligated to call due to favorable pot odds or the relatively large amount of money at stake.

get picked off: Get caught bluffing (and lose the pot). "Tully picked him off when he tried to bluff on the river." See SNAPPED OFF.

get played with: Have an opponent call one's bet or raise.

get the best of it: Have a hand or be in a situation that is favored to win.

◆

get the right price: When a sufficient amount of money is in the pot to make a call or raise profitable in the long run.

get the worst of it: See WORST OF IT.

get well: Break even or go ahead after losing.

give a card: GIVE A FREE CARD.

give action: 1. Bet or raise, or call a bet or raise, particularly when a hand is an underdog to win the pot. **2.** In general, gamble with someone, usually in a poker game. "You'll like playing with John. He gives action."

give a free card: Check and allow opponents to see another card without having to put any bets into the pot. See FREE CARD.

give a hand away: Play a hand in such an obvious manner that opponents are able to guess the value of the cards.

give credit (to, for): Assume that a player has a hand of a certain strength. "When he went all in, I gave him credit for the full house and folded." Also see PUT A PLAYER ON A HAND.

go all in: Bet all one's chips.

go both ways: In high-low games, go for both the high end and low end of the pot.

going high: In high-low games, competing for the high end of the pot.

going home hand: A hand to which a player has all his chips committed; if he loses, he's busted and is going home.

going low: In high-low games, competing for the low end of the pot.

go into the tank: See INTO THE TANK.

gold bracelet: See BRACELET.

gone goose: 1. A player holding a losing hand. **2.** A player who has already lost.

good: 1. The winning hand, for example, one player saying to another on the showdown, "It's good." **2.** A relatively strong hand. **3.** Having skills, as in *a good player*.

good action: A game with lots of betting and good-sized pots.

"Good call": A compliment one player gives to another after a difficult or gutsy call of a large bet or raise, particularly if the bettor was bluffing.

good fold: See GOOD LAYDOWN.

good game: 1. A game that is likely to be profitable due to weaker opposition. **2.** A game that is run efficiently or that is enjoyable to play. **3.** Having good skills. "Johnny plays a good game of high-limit."

"Good hand": An often-heard compliment given by one player to another after a nice-sized pot has been won. Also, *"Nice hand."*

good laydown: 1. Folding a strong hand against an opponent's bigger hand when that opponent makes a large bet. **2.** What one player might say to another when this occurs.

good luck: 1. Good fortune that occurs in a manner greater than random chance would suggest. **2.** When spoken, wishing someone this condition.

good one: A card that improves one's hand.

good percentage play: A play that is mathematically sound, and will show a profit in the long run.

good run: A series of plays or sessions that end favorably. Also, *winning streak.* Opposite of *bad run* or *bad streak.*

good streak: GOOD RUN.

gorillas: In hold'em, hole cards of two kings (comes from the *K*'s in King Kong).

got all the money in: To put all one's chips into the pot. "Did he get all his money in before the flop or after?"

got broke: To lose all one's money. "I got broke when my opponent rivered a full house against my nut flush."

got loser: A player who is losing or who has lost.

go to war: 1. Play a hand for the maximum number of bets it takes to get to the showdown. "We both flopped sets and went to war." **2.** Play aggressively in an all-out style.

go to your pocket: Take more cash out after big losses deplete or bankrupt your table bankroll.

grand: $1,000, usually expressed as *one grand*.

graveyard: Graveyard shift.

graveyard shift: The overnight shift in a cardroom or casino. Also, *night shift*.

gravy: 1. Extra, usually unexpected, profit on a hand or in a game. "I got two overcalls. That was all gravy." **2.** The amount a player is ahead. "I'm in a thousand; the rest is gravy."

green chip: $25 chip (so named because it is typically green in color). Also Quarter.

grind: Play long hours and earn relatively little for the effort.

grinder: One who plays long hours, often in low-limit games, and earns relatively little for the effort.

gut: The inside, missing part of a straight draw. A jack would be the *gut* in the hand 8-9-10-Q.

guts: Attribute of a player with no fear.

gutshot: INSIDE STRAIGHT.

gutshot straight: INSIDE STRAIGHT.

gypsy in: When the big blind gets to see the flop without extra cost because no raises precede his position—as opposed to variations in which players must raise the big blind to enter the pot, thereby forcing the big blind to meet that raise to stay active in the pot.

h: Symbol for hearts in written text. 8h is the 8♥.

half-bet: In a limit game, the difference in size between the big blind and the small blind bet in a 1-2 type structure ($1/$2, $3/$6, $20/$40, etc.). "The little blind might call the half-bet in a 1-2 chip structure with any decent hand."

half-kill game: A limit poker variation in which the stakes increase by 50% on the next hand when two pots in a row are won by the same player or, in high-low games, when a SCOOPED POT of at least a specified size occurs. Compare to KILL GAME.

half the pot: 1. In high-low games, the portion of the pot that either the best high hand or the best low hand wins. **2.** In other games, players with tied hands split the pot, getting 50% each.

halved: Split the pot with another player (usually used in HIGH-LOW games).

hammer: 1. The threat or potential of a big raise or all-in bet. **2.** Make a big raise or an all-in bet in no-limit hold'em. **3.** Use the leverage of a big stack or late position to bully opponents with aggressive play.

hand: 1. The cards a player holds. **2.** Specifically good cards. "I folded because I put him on a hand that time." **3.** The best five cards a player holds in games where more than five cards are available in which to form a hand, such as in hold'em, Omaha, or seven-card stud. **4.** Having cards, as in *to be dealt a hand of poker*. **5.** The interval from shuffle to shuffle. "Who won the last hand?"

hand-dominated: A game, such as Omaha, in which the strength of a player's cards is relatively more important in strategy considerations than in variations such as hold'em and draw poker, in which a player's POSITION carries greater weight.

hand for hand: The situation that arises when players are ON THE BUBBLE in a tournament and all dealers are instructed to wait after completion of their hands before another round of cards is dealt so that each table will play one hand at a time until a player busts out, meaning that the remaining players receive prize money. This can also occur when the FINAL TABLE will be assembled after the loss of one more player or when prize money increases substantially with the elimination of one more player.

hand is good: 1. The winning hand. **2.** What one player may say to an opponent when an opponent has a better hand.

handle: The unique name by which a player gains access to an ONLINE CARDROOM and also by which he is identified. Also, *user name*.

hand reading: Being perceptive and able to analyze the hand likely to be held by an opponent.

hand selection: In general, the starting cards a player chooses to play.

hand value: The strength of a hand.

hard: In a cash transaction, the amount of money a player buys as chips. For example, a player may give a CHIP RUNNER a $100 bill and ask for $50 *hard* (chips) and the rest SOFT (cash).

have the best of it: See BEST OF IT.

have the worst of it: See WORST OF IT.

heads-up: HEAD TO HEAD.

head to head: 1. Poker played by two players only, one against the other. **2.** A pot contested by two players. Also, *heads-up*.

heart: 1. A card in the hearts suit. **2.** What a player with the courage to call or initiate big bets or raises with speculative hands has.

hearts: One of the four suits in a deck of cards, using a red heart symbol (♥) consisting of 13 cards, 2-3-4-5-6-7-8-9-10-J-Q-K-A.

heat: 1. Pressure put on another player through heavy betting. **2.** Unwanted attention of cardroom supervisors due to disallowed, disruptive, or illegal play. "That thief brings heat on himself just by sitting down at a table."

◆

hedge bet: A bet made on the side as insurance to limit losses on a poker hand, game, or tournament.

help: 1. A card or cards that improve a hand. Often part of the phrase *get help*. **2.** When a hand improves with a fortuitous draw. "He was looking for help on the turn."

hidden hand: 1. In a stud game, a hand whose strength is not evident to opponents. **2.** A hand played in such a way that opponents are misled into thinking that the player has a hand of much lesser value. See CONCEALED.

high: 1. Short for *high poker*, the typical version of poker played in which the highest-ranked hand wins. **2.** In a game of HIGH-LOW, the name for the part of the pot that goes to the best high hand. When announced or declared, usually preceded by *go* or *going*. "I'm going high," Jo-Jo declared at the showdown, revealing trip aces. **3.** A game played for large amounts, particularly as part of the phrase *high stakes* (as opposed to medium or low stakes). **4.** In high poker, the best hand. **5.** The connecting term in the naming of a high card to a hand, as in a *king-high straight* or an *ace-high* hand.

◆

high card: 1. The highest-ranked of cards randomly drawn. For example, if king, jack, 7 and 5 were drawn, the king would be the high card. If the next card was an ace, then the ace would be the high card. **2.** The poker hand that has no higher-ranking combinations, such as a pair, two pair, or better; basically five odd cards. Such a hand is named by its highest-ranking card. For example, 3-9-K-7-10 is a *king-high* hand. Also called *no pair*.

high draw: 1. In a high-low game, going for the high half of the pot with a drawing hand, such as four cards to a straight or flush. **2.** The game HIGH DRAW POKER. **3.** A run of consecutive high-ranked cards needing one more card to complete, such as 9-10-J-Q.

high draw poker: Standard DRAW POKER in which the highest-ranked card wins.

high end: HIGH HALF.

high half: In HIGH-LOW games, the part of the pot that goes to the best high hand. Also, *high end*.

high hand: 1. The best hand in high or HIGH-LOW poker. **2.** A hand going for the high half of the pot in high-low.

high limit: Poker played for large sums of money; usually indicates games with limits of $50/$100 and higher. Also *large limit*, *high stakes*.

high-low: Poker variation in which players compete for the best high and low hands, with the winner of each getting half the pot. If one hand is both the best high and the best low, that hand wins the entire pot. Sometimes called *high-low split*.

high-low split: HIGH-LOW.

high on board: In stud games, having the highest-ranked card or hand on BOARD.

high poker: See HIGH.

high roller: A gambler who bets large sums of money.

high spade in hole: Seven-card stud variation in which the player holding the highest spade as a downcard splits the pot with the best high hand.

high stakes: See HIGH LIMIT.

hi-lo: A variant spelling of HIGH-LOW.

hit: 1. Improve a hand with a fortuitous draw. "Frankie hit the flush on the river and busted me." **2.** A hand that gets hurt by a bad draw **3.** Take a big loss. "I took a huge hit when my nut flush got rivered by a full." **4.** Draw additional cards in draw poker.

hit a hand: Make a strong hand when a new card or cards are drawn.

hit-and-run artist: A player who gambles for a relatively short time and leaves with winnings.

hitchhiker: 1. In HIGH-LOW, an opponent who is going for the same high or low half of the pot as another player, while at least one player is going for the opposite half of the pot. **2.** An extra player who comes into a pot. "When I raised John, he called and I also got two hitchhikers."

hit it bigger: Improve a hand such that it becomes of greater strength than that of an opponent.

hit the flop: In hold'em and Omaha, a hand which is greatly improved by the three-card flop.

hit your draw: Get a fifth card to make a straight or flush.

H.O.E.: A game with rounds rotating among three variations, limit hold'em, Omaha 8-or-better, and seven-card stud 8-or-better. Typically each variation lasts for one round of cards; sometimes, for a specified time limit such as thirty minutes.

hold'em: A high poker game featuring two starting down cards, a FLOP of three shared COMMUNITY CARDS, a fourth community card (the TURN), and then a fifth (the RIVER), with four betting rounds. At the showdown, any combination of the best five out of the seven available cards wins the pot. The "official" name of the game is *Texas hold'em*.

hold up: For the best hand before the end to go on and win.

hole: 1. A weakness in a player's game. **2.** In stud variations, the concealed cards held by a player. **3.** When part of the phrase *in the hole*, a player who is losing money in a game or overall. "I'm in the hole $400." Also see STUCK.

hole card: A card held face down by a player, the value of which is hidden from other players. Also, DOWNCARD, *pocket card*.

Hollywood: Show off or act in a grandiose manner, sometimes with respect to trying to influence the actions of opponents during a betting situation.

home game: 1. A poker game restricted to invited members or held in a noncommercial poker room, as opposed to a PUBLIC GAME, which is open to any players of legal age who wish to play. Also, *private game*. **2.** A nonstandard poker variation, such as Anaconda or spit-in-the-ocean, found only in home games.

home poker: 1. Poker played in someone's house. **2.** HOME GAME, definition 2.

honest: 1. A bet that is backed by a strong hand, as opposed to a bluff, which is backed by weak cards that probably won't win if there is a showdown. **2.** Part of the phrase KEEP SOMEONE HONEST. **3.** An individual who plays a fair game and abides by the rules. **4.** A poker game fairly dealt and played, as opposed to one in which cheats operate.

H.O.R.S.E.: A game with rounds rotating among five variations, limit hold'em, Omaha 8-or-better, razz, seven-card stud high, and seven-card stud 8-or-better. Typically each variation lasts for one round of cards; sometimes, for a specified time limit.

horse: A player being staked in a game or tournament for a percentage of the profits. *I busted out after a few hours, but my horse is one of the chip leaders in the tournament and running strong.*

Horseshoe Casino: The legendary gaming establishment in downtown Las Vegas, the world's most famous poker venue. The Horseshoe is the birthplace of the World Series of Poker, originally run by the Binion family until its purchase in 2004 by Harrah's, when it was renamed to Binion's.

H.O.S.: A game with rounds rotating among three variations, limit hold'em, Omaha 8-or-better, and seven-card stud high. Typically each variation lasts for one round of cards; sometimes, for a specified time limit.

H.O.S.E.: A game with rounds rotating among four variations, limit hold'em, Omaha 8-or-better, seven-card stud high, and seven-card stud 8-or-better. Typically each variation lasts for one round of cards; sometimes, for a specified time limit.

hot: 1. A player who is winning many pots. **2.** A player who has become angry. "Johnson got real hot when Wolfie drew a third cowboy on the river and busted his pocket rockets."

hot hand: A player on a winning streak.

hot streak: WINNING STREAK. The opposite is a *bad streak* or *bad run*, in which many losses are incurred.

hourly rate: 1. The amount of money players are charged per hour to play cards, often called the RAKE. **2.** The amount of money, on average, that a player wins or loses per hour.

house: 1. Casino, cardroom, or venue that hosts gambling games. **2.** Short for FULL HOUSE. "The third three on board gave him a house."

house cut: 1. RAKE. **2.** In house-banked games, the advantage a casino enjoys or the percentage amount it wins on every hand. Also *house edge, house percentage*.

house edge: HOUSE CUT, definition 2.

house percentage: HOUSE CUT, definition 2.

house player: An individual employed by a casino to play and give action to a game; SHILL.

house rules: 1. The agreed-upon rules for playing games. **2.** The accepted standards of play as established by a cardroom, casino, or private game for play in its games. Also *rules*, *rules of the game*.

"How deep are you?": A request to a player of how many chips he has. Also, "How much you got?"

"How much you got?": "How deep are you?"

hustle: 1. Work hard to win money or to make a living. **2.** Use unethical or unfair methods to separate naïve or unsuspecting players from their money.

hustler: 1. A con artist who uses unethical or unfair methods to dupe naïve or unsuspecting players out of their money. **2.** A resourceful and honest player who works hard to make his living or win money.

idiot end of a straight: Ignorant end of a straight.

ignorant end of a straight: In hold'em, the lowest possible straight based on the cards on the board. For example, a player holding a 3 with a board of 4-5-6-7 has the *ignorant end of a straight*, which might be a problem since an opponent holding an 8 would have a higher and winning straight. Also, *bottom end of a straight*. Opposite of TOP END OF A STRAIGHT.

illegal bet: A wager that is against the rules and not valid, as opposed to a *legal bet*, which is acceptable and binding.

immortal: A perfect or unbeatable hand.

implied odds: The amount of money that can potentially be won (assuming opponents will make additional bets) compared to the cost of a bet. For example, if a player is contemplating calling a $10,000 bet, and he figures that $90,000 more will be put into the pot, he has implied odds of 9 to 1—that is, he is betting $10,000 to win $90,000. Also called EFFECTIVE ODDS.

improve: With respect to a hand, become stronger due to a good card or cards being drawn.

in a pot: Actively competing for a pot, that is, not having folded.

in back: In LATE POSITION.

in-between hands: MARGINAL HANDS.

in for: The number of chips or amount of money a player has committed to a pot or game. "Hey Joe, how much you in for in the game?"

in front: **1.** The amount a player is winning or the situation of winning. "How much are you in front?" "Are you in front?" **2.** Being in early POSITION on a hand. **3.** A position that is before another player. "I was in front of Chris and he kept raising me."

in position: Being in late POSITION, that is, being one of the last players to act in a round.

inside: **1.** Being an employee of a cardroom, used in phrases such as *he works inside* and *he works on the inside*. **2.** Being part of a team or group with particular knowledge or access, as part of the phrase *he's on the inside*. **3.** INSIDE STRAIGHT.

inside gambler: A gambler who works for or in a casino and hosts games for other players.

inside straight: 1. A STRAIGHT draw consisting of four cards with one "hole," such that only one rank can complete the hand, for example, 2-4-5-6, in which only a 3 can complete the straight. Also *belly buster, gutshot straight, gutshot, one-gapper.* Compare to an OPEN-ENDED STRAIGHT or *outside draw*, which has two ranks (eight OUTS) to complete. **2.** The completion of such a draw. "My set got beat by an inside straight."

inside wrap: In Omaha, a straight draw that lies between the highest and lowest board cards, such as holding K-Q-J-8 with an A-10-2 flop.

insurance: A side bet made on the possible occurrence of cards being drawn or hands being completed, typically made to cover a player's risk of losing a pot, and usually made with some player other than one involved in the pot.

in the air: 1. Cards already being dealt, meaning that a hand is in progress and will be completed. **2.** The starting time for a game or tournament. "The cards will be in the air at noon."

in the blind: Making a betting choice—check, bet, or raise—without looking at newly dealt cards. Also, *in the dark.*

in the chips: 1. Winning. **2.** Having lots of money. "It's no coincidence. Louie's been in the chips since he got away from the craps table."

in the dark: IN THE BLIND.

in the hole: 1. Cards held face down by a player in a stud or flop game. **2.** To be losing and having a long way to go to break even. Also, *stuck*.

in the middle: 1. A player located between a bettor and a raiser. **2.** Being in MIDDLE POSITION. **3.** The pot. "My full house gave me all the chips in the middle."

in the money: 1. In a tournament, to finish among the top players and win cash. The terms *money finish* and *cashed* are related. **2.** A player loaded with money.

in turn: Playing in the correct order of action as required by the rules, as opposed to OUT OF TURN.

Internet player: 1. An individual who plays poker on the Internet. **2.** A derogatory term used by cash and tournament competitors for players who have learned their poker skills on the Internet and are viewed as poor players.

Internet poker: ONLINE POKER.

in the tank: INTO THE TANK. "It's a tough decision and he's in the tank."

into the tank: Being deep in thought on a decisive play. Usually part of the phrase *go into the tank*.

into the think tank: INTO THE TANK.

invest: The amount of money bet into a pot or put at risk in a game.

involved: 1. Being in competition for a pot. **2.** Having called or made bets to stay active in a pot.

IOU: Literally, *I owe you*. Money borrowed that needs to be paid back.

isolate: Raise with the intention of creating a heads-up situation.

"It's good": What one player says to another when the opponent's hand is the winner. "Big Cat mucked his cards on the river and said, 'It's good, take the pot.'"

J: Symbol used in written text for a jack in any suit.

jack: The lowest-ranking of the FACE CARDS, with a stylized image of a man on it and the letter J, of which a deck contains four, one in each suit. An old name for the jack is *knave*.

jack it up: 1. Raise a bet. "I'm going to jack it up" means "I raise." **2.** Raise the stakes of a game. "How about we jack up the limit to $10/$20?"

jackpot: A bonus given by cardrooms for losers of powerful hands (with certain restrictions), usually aces full or better losing to four of a kind or better hands. This bonus is often split with the largest share going to the loser of the hand, the next larger share to the winner, and some remaining share being split among the remaining players at the table. Also, *bad beat jackpot*.

jackpots: Another name for JACKS OR BETTER.

jacks: A pair of jacks.

jacks or better: FIVE-CARD DRAW in which a player must have at least a pair of jacks to make an opening bet in the first round.

jack up: JACK IT UP.

jam: 1. Bet and raise aggressively or the maximum amount possible, often part of the phrase *ram and jam.* **2.** Push all one's chips into the pot. **3.** When the maximum number of raises have been reached. **4.** Complete the hand being played for. "I jammed the straight."

jammed pot: 1. A pot that has been raised the maximum number of times allowed. **2.** A pot in which two or more players are raising and reraising.

Jesse James: In hold'em, hole cards of 4-5.

John: A weak or naïve player who is a mark for better players or cheats (comes from the term prostitutes call their customers).

joint: Any gambling establishment. Also *casino, cardroom, house.*

◆

joker: An extra card or cards in the deck, often bearing a picture of a court jester or similar figure; sometimes called the *53rd card* in the deck. The joker is not used in most cardroom poker games. When it is incorporated into a game, it usually has some properties of a wild card, as described under BUG, or the full properties of a wild card as described under WILD CARD.

joker poker: Poker played with a joker used as a wild card (usually a BUG).

joker wild: A game in which the joker can be used as a card of any rank or value (as opposed to a BUG).

juice: 1. Influence exerted by a person with power. "BB gets into any restaurant or club he wants; he has a lot of juice in Vegas." Also, *pull*. **2.** RAKE.

juice joint: A gaming establishment that cheats, or is full of thieves.

K: Symbol used in written text for a king in any suit.

Kansas City lowball: DEUCE-TO-SEVEN.

keep someone honest: When holding a marginal hand, call the final bet of a player one suspects to be bluffing.

keep someone in line: Raise or reraise an aggressive player to keep him from bullying and controlling play.

key hand: A significant hand that marked a reversal in fortunes, changed the way things were going, or was the most important hand in a session.

kibitzer: A spectator who watches the action, often one who talks too much and offers unsolicited and unwanted comments about the ongoing action.

kicker: The highest side card to any hand of one pair, two pair, three of a kind, or rarely, four of a kind hand. For example, a player holding 3-3-5-7-A has a pair of threes with an ace kicker. In hold'em, with competing pocket cards of A-J and K-J on a flop of J-Q-3-J-4, the pot would be won by the A-J hand, the three jacks with the ace kicker beating the three jacks with the king kicker.

kicker trouble: Having the auxiliary card to a pair (the KICKER) be of weaker potential than another player's side card. For example, with a flop of A-10-5, a player with A-J has *kicker trouble* against any A-K or A-Q hand. Unless a jack flops (or a king and a queen come in succession), the A-J hand would lose.

kill: 1. Render a hand DEAD and not in play. **2.** Win lots of money from an opponent or a game. **3.** Put in the required extra blind in a KILL GAME.

kill button: A plastic disk used to indicate that a player qualifies for a kill and is required to kill the pot on the following deal. See KILL GAME.

killed: 1. Losing decisively. "I got killed in that game." **2.** A hand that become worthless. **3.** A pot with a KILL bet.

kill game: A variation in which the winner of two pots in a row or, in high-low games, of a SCOOPED POT of a specified size, puts in an extra blind double the size of the big blind on the following pot and where the stakes double on the next hand for all players. Sometimes called *full-kill game*, to contrast with HALF-KILL GAME.

kill poker: KILL GAME.

kill pot: A pot in which the stakes are doubled as described under KILL GAME.

king: The highest-ranking of the FACE CARDS, with a stylized image of a king on it and the letter K, of which a deck contains four, one in each suit. Also, *cowboy*.

kings: A pair of kings.

kitty: In private poker games, money taken from the pot to be kept separately and used for other purposes (such as refreshments) by the participants.

knave: An old name for a JACK.

knock: Check.

knock out: 1. Eliminate a player from a tournament. **2.** In a cash game, bankrupt an opponent.

large: 1. A big bet, a game played for high stakes, or a situation or risk that is substantial. **2.** A term for $1,000. "Jones sat down with nine large in the $100/$200 game."

large bet: 1. A bet in LIMIT POKER that is in the higher tier of the betting limit, for example, the $60 bet in a $30/$60 game. **2.** In pot-limit and no-limit, a bet that is of greater size than normal.

large-buy-in tournament: BIG BUY-IN TOURNAMENT.

large field: A relatively large number of players in a tournament.

large limit: Poker played for large sums of money. Also *high limit, big limit*.

last longer bet: A wager between two or more players on who will go further in a tournament before being eliminated, the winner being the last active player among the participants who has not yet busted out.

last to act: The player who acts last in a betting round.

late position: The last two or three seats in a nine- or 10-handed game, or the last or next-to-last player in a game with five to seven players.

late steal position: The position of being one of the last players to act in the first round, in which the leverage of having the last or next to last action can be used to force opponents to fold with aggressive betting and thus win the blinds by default.

lay it down: Fold. "Buster had two pair, but when he got raised, he decided to lay it down."

laydown: The act of folding, often implying folding a good hand in the face of pressure.

lay down: Fold.

lay odds: Bet the favorite by putting more money at stake than will be won if the wager succeeds. For example, if odds are laid at 1 to 2, then a bet of $20 would win $10.

lead: 1. Make the initial bet in a round. "I throw my marginal hands away when an early position player leads at the pot." Also, *take the lead.* **2.** Act from early position. **3.** A hand that is better than others before the showdown. "John's set was in the lead right to the river." **4.** In a tournament, a player with more chips than his opponents. **5.** The player who makes the first bet.

lead at the pot: In a betting round, put the first bet into the pot.

leader: 1. The player making the first bet in a round. **2.** In a tournament, the player with the most chips.

leading: 1. With more cards still to be drawn, a hand that is higher ranked than an opponent's. **2.** The player betting first in a round.

leak: 1. A weakness or "hole" in a player's game. **2.** An activity away from the poker tables that drains one's bankroll, such as craps or sports betting.

leather ass: A TIGHT player; ROCK.

legal bet: A wager that is within the rules and is acceptable, as opposed to an ILLEGAL BET, which is not valid.

legitimate hand: A hand that is of reasonable strength, as opposed to a BLUFF, in which the hand held is weak.

leg up: 1. In a KILL game in which players kill who win two pots in a row, having won the previous pot and being required to kill the pot if the subsequent pot is won. **2.** Having an advantage over an opponent or situation. In both meanings, usually part of the phrase *have a leg up*.

level: 1. ROUND, definition 1. **2.** The relative skill level of a player or, in general, of a game.

light: To not put enough chips in the pot on a called or required bet, or forgetting to post an ante or blind, and thus owing more chips to the pot. A dealer might tell a player "You're $20 light on the bet." If everyone hasn't put in an ante, a player might say, "Who's light in the pot?" Also *short, shy*.

light action: A game with relatively modest betting, much less than the normal amount, as opposed to one with HEAVY ACTION, in which there is much betting and raising.

limit: 1. The bet size permitted in a game. Also, *betting limit*. **2.** A shortening of LIMIT POKER. "Is this a no-limit game?" "No, we're playing limit."

limit poker: The type of betting structure for poker games in which the minimum and maximum bet sizes are set at fixed amounts, for example, a $5/$10 game, in which bets or raises are all in increments of $5 in early specified betting rounds and in increments of $10 in later specified betting rounds. Compare with POT LIMIT and NO LIMIT, in which, in the former, bets are limited by the size of the pot, and in the latter, bets can be as large as a player desires up to the as much he has in front of him.

limit stakes: LIMIT POKER.

limp: Call a bet, that is, not raise, as a way to enter the pot cheaply, or, if the first player to make a bet, open for the minimum. Also, *limp in*.

limper: A player who makes the minimum permitted bet as a way to enter the pot.

limp in: LIMP.

little: Short for the LITTLE BLIND or the little blind bet.

little bet: The small bet in LIMIT POKER (before the second level in a two-tier structure is reached), as for example, the $5 bet in a $5/$10 game.

little blind: SMALL BLIND.

little card: 1. In high poker, a 2, 3, 4, 5, 6, or 7. **2.** In ACE-TO-FIVE low poker, an ace 2, 3, 4 or 5. **3.** In DEUCE-TO-SEVEN low poker, a 2, 3, 4, 5, 6, or 7. Also, *small card*. Compare to BIG CARD, MEDIUM CARD.

live: 1. A hand that is ACTIVE (not folded), and still in contention for a pot. **2.** Cards that have not yet been played and are still available to be drawn. **3.** A legal hand or card that has not been ruled DEAD (due to an irregularity). **4.** A game with lots of action. **5.** A poker game that is played face-to-face, as opposed to being played online.

live blind: A BLIND position that has the option to raise the pot when the betting comes back around, typical in most hold'em and Omaha games. Compare to DEAD BLIND.

live cards: Cards that have not been seen and are still available to be drawn.

---

live game: 1. A cash poker game in progress. **2.** A game with good action. **3.** A game played by players who are physically present around a table as opposed to games played on the Internet.

live hand: A player or his cards that are still ACTIVE (not folded) and in contention for the pot.

live one: A player with relatively poor skills who provides money for better players to win. Also *fish, producer, customer, provider, sucker*.

live straddle: See STRADDLE.

loan shark: A moneylender who charges interest (usually at extortionate rates). Also, *Shylock*.

loball: A variant spelling of LOWBALL.

local: A player who lives in the vicinity of a cardroom or casino and is a regular player.

lock: 1. A hand or situation that cannot lose or is perceived that way. **2.** Put a hold on a seat when on a waiting list. "Lock that seat for Georgie."

locked up: 1. In high-low, having the high, low, or both ends already won before the showdown. **2.** Chips held by a tight player that are difficult to pry loose. **3.** A seat that is reserved. See LOCK UP.

lock up: Reserve a seat for a filled poker game and once it becomes available, be given extra time to claim it.

log on: 1. Obtain access to an online site by using an identifying name and password that is unique to the user. **2.** Obtain access to the internet

long call: 1. Calling with a hand, usually on the last round, with cards that appear to be a longshot to win. **2.** Taking a long time to call a bet (and usually indicating a difficult decision).

long run: The concept of expected results occurring over a large number of trials.

longshot: A hand or situation that will rarely win or occur.

look someone up: Call a bet on the end with cards that can beat only a bluff.

loose: 1. A player who plays many hands and enters many pots. **2.** When applied to a game, a collection of players who play many pots.

loose call: An unsound call of a bet or raise.

loose-aggressive: Players who not only play many hands but play them aggressively with frequent bets and raises.

loosey-goosey: A loose player, one who plays too many hands.

lose: 1. Get beat in a hand or in a game; not win a pot. **2.** Have less money in a cash game than when one started. **3.** Fail to achieve a desired result. **4.** In a tournament, fail to win or fail to earn money.

loser: 1. In either one session or overall, a player whose bankroll is smaller than when he started (as apposed to WINNER). "The cards just aren't hitting me. I'm loser over the last month." **2.** A player who is not winning or did not win in a game or tournament. **3.** A hand that is unlikely to win. **4.** An individual whose personality is not liked or respected—*that guy's a loser.*

losing streak: A series of plays or sessions that result in losses, as opposed to WINNING STREAK. Also, *bad run*.

low: 1. Short for LOW POKER or LOWBALL, the version of poker played in which the lowest hand wins (as opposed to HIGH or HIGH POKER). **2.** In a game of HIGH-LOW, the part of the pot that goes to the best low hand; when announced or declared, usually preceded by *go* or *going:* "I'm going low," Fred declared at the showdown. **3.** With respect to a betting structure in a LIMIT game, the lower amount of a two-tier structure, for example, the $5 betting rounds in a $5/$10 game. **4:** Game played for small amounts (as opposed to medium or high stakes)—LOW STAKES. **5.** In high poker, the weakest of the hands.

lowball: A poker variation, usually of FIVE-CARD DRAW, played in which the best low hand wins. Sometimes called *lowball draw* or *draw lowball*.

lowball draw: LOWBALL.

low end: LOW HALF.

low half: In HIGH-LOW games, the part of the pot that goes to the best low hand.

---

low hand: 1. The best low hand in HIGH-LOW games. **2.** The hand held by a player going for the low half of the pot in HIGH-LOW games, or the holder of that hand.

low limit: Poker played for small sums of money. Also, *small limit*.

low poker: Any form of poker in which the lowest-ranked hand wins, as LOWBALL or RAZZ.

low stakes: Game or games played for relatively small sums of money; usually indicates games with limits smaller than $10/$20.

luck: 1. Good fortune that occurs more often than random chance or experience would suggest. **2.** Chance that could occur in either a good way or a bad way.

luck out: 1. Win when the expectation is to lose. **2.** Be fortunate in a situation.

lucky: 1. Being fortunate in a specific or general way. **2.** Winning or succeeding in situations more than would be reasonably expected.

lucky draw: Catching one or more cards that are mathematically unlikely and that improve a hand to a winner or likely winner.

lying: Bluffing; representing a hand that is not actually held.

lying in the bushes: Setting a trap with a very strong but disguised hand against opponents who do not suspect the actual hand strength. See SLOWPLAY.

made hand: A five-card completed hand; in high poker, usually a straight or better (as opposed to a DRAWING HAND), and in low poker, usually an 8 or better. Also, COMPLETE HAND.

main event: The big, prestigious event in a multi-event tournament, usually the largest buy-in no-limit hold'em tournament and often the last event held.

main game: 1. In a cardroom, the highest-stakes game and often the one in which the best players compete. **2.** With multiple games of the same variety and limit, the one toward which players are requested to move from a MUST-MOVE game as seats open.

main pot: When a player is ALL IN and two or more competing players still have chips, the original pot containing the matched bets and raises of all players, as opposed to SIDE POT, a segregated pot created for the players who still have chips to wager.

make: 1. Complete a drawing hand (such as getting an 8 to fill a 9-10-J-Q straight draw) or complete any hand that a player is going for (such as drawing a jack to a hand of J-J-Q-Q, to make a full house of jacks over queens). **2.** Be discovered when trying to hide behind a disguise or be undercover, usually said of a thief. "The tall fella, who had perfect recall, made the cardsharp as soon as he began to shuffle, despite the man's beard."

make a hand: Improve to a hand that will probably win.

make a move at the pot: Bet with the intention of forcing opponents to fold and thus winning the pot by default.

make a play: 1. Bet or raise with weak cards with the intention of bluffing opponents out of a pot; bluff. **2.** Bet strongly hoping that opponents will fold and the pot can be won by default.

make bank on: Make a bet with an expected positive outcome.

maniac: A player who bets and raises recklessly.

marginal hands: Hands that are borderline profitable, with long-term expectations of about break-even when played, thus being about equally correct to play as to fold. Also, *in-between hands*.

mark: 1. A player who is targeted by cheats. **2.** Something found on the back of a card that is disfigured through use, making the card recognizable by players. **3.** Illegally and subtly alter the back surface of the playing cards so that their value can be determined by the manipulator.

marker: 1. In a cardroom or casino, a slip of paper indicating an advance or loan, which is signed by a player when the casino advances him money. **2.** An IOU. Among players or loan sharks, this is usually a more casual handshake agreement.

marks: See MARK, definition 2.

massive-field tournament: A tournament of 1,000 or more players.

match the pot: Bet the same amount as the total already in the pot.

maximum value: To induce from opponents the most bets possible on a winning hand, often used as part of the expression, "get maximum value."

mechanic: A card magician or CHEAT, one who is expert at manipulating cards in a nonrandom manner.

mechanic's grip: A manner of holding cards that makes it easy to manipulate them for card tricks or to cheat.

medium-action tournament: A tournament with levels of more than twenty minutes and less than one hour.

medium buy-in tournament: A tournament which costs from $200 to under $1,000 to enter.

medium card: 1. In high poker, a 10, 9, 8, and sometimes, a 7 or 6. **2.** In ACE-TO-FIVE low poker, a 10, 9, 8, 7, or 6. **3.** In DEUCE-TO-SEVEN low poker, a 10, 9, or 8.

medium-field tournament: A tournament of 100 to 200 players.

medium limit: Poker played for relatively moderate stakes, neither high nor low; usually indicates games with limits of $10/$20 up to $40/$80.

medium suited connectors: Two cards, either the 7-8, 8-9, 9-10, or 10-J, that are of consecutive rank and in the same suit.

meet: Call or match a bet. "I'll meet that $25 and go one better—raise!"

Mexican bankroll: A wad of cash with a big bill on the outside and small bills on the inside.

Mexican standoff: A tie, a pot that is split.

Mickey Mouse: 1. A derogatory term to describe a game too small and not worth playing. **2.** Anything poorly and unprofessionally done.

middle: 1. The MAIN POT when a SIDE POT has been created. "Those chips go in the middle." **2.** The inside part or GAP of an INSIDE STRAIGHT. **3.** The pot.

middle cards: In HIGH-LOW games, cards that are neither strong low cards or strong high ones, often referring to 7, 8, 9 and 10 (and sometimes 6 and jack), such that these cards, combined with others of like nature, have little value toward winning either the high or low end of the pot.

middle position: 1. The middle three or four seats in a nine- or 10-handed game or the middle position in a smaller game. **2.** In a pot contested by three players, the second to act.

milk a game: Play tight and slowly extract profits from a game.

miscall: At the showdown, incorrectly announce the ranking of a hand. See OVERCALL.

misdeal: 1. A deal deemed illegal and therefore invalid. **2.** Deal a hand in a way that involves an irregularity, such that a misdeal is declared.

misread: 1. Erroneously read a hand, for example, think 4-5-6-7-9 is a straight when it is just a 9-high hand. **2.** Think an opponent has a hand considerably different, either stronger, weaker, or of a different type, from what he actually holds.

misread the board: In hold'em and Omaha, wrongly calculate the strength of a hand in relation to the board or erroneously read the board. For example, in Omaha, in which misreading the board is common, a player holding 2-7-K-K with a board of 3-4-5-6-Q may mistakenly think he has a straight, but since he must play two of his pocket cards, in reality he has only a pair of kings.

miss: Not make the hand one is trying for. "On the river, a spade came and Big Bob missed his diamond flush draw."

miss the blind: Be away from a table when it is time to put in the BLIND. (In a tournament, have the blind posted in a player's absence and forfeited to the winner of the pot).

miss the flop: When a player's starting cards are not improved by the three community cards of the flop. "Jack's 3-3 missed the A-9-9 flop and he folded when T-Mart pushed in $2,000."

mixed game: Multiple poker variations alternated as part of the game structure, for example, H.O.R.S.E.

money bubble: BUBBLE.

money finish: 1. Ending a tournament among the top players, and thus winning a cash prize. The terms *in the money* and *cashed* are related. **2.** Having a big finish in a game and coming out with good profits.

money flow: The pattern in which money moves around in a poker game.

money management: A strategy used by smart players to preserve their capital, manage their wins, and avoid unnecessary risks and big losses.

money player: 1. A player who performs well under pressure, such as when stakes are highest. **2.** A player who mostly plays cash games as opposed to tournaments.

"Money plays": An announcement by a dealer or floorperson that a player is betting cash and it is a valid and legal wager for the game.

monkey flush: A three-card flush.

monster: A very big poker hand.

Montana banana: In hold'em, hole cards of 2-9.

morning glory: A weak player who plays too many inferior hands but still wins lots of chips early in a poker session, only to have luck even out and lose all his chips back after some time.

mortal nuts: Given the cards on board, the best possible hand at the moment, and likely the best even with cards to come. Depending on the situation, might be slightly *better* than the NUTS.

mouth bet: ORAL BET.

move someone off the pot: Cause a player to fold by forceful betting or raising. "Finny got Sally to move off the pot when he bet $2,000 on the turn."

move in: Go ALL IN on a bet or raise, putting all one's chips at stake.

moves: Fancy plays: bluffs. "Watch out for B-Man; he's got lots of moves."

muck: 1. Fold. "He bet and I mucked." **2.** The place on the table where discarded cards are placed. "Throw that piece of cheese in the muck."

multiple rebuy tournament: A REBUY TOURNAMENT that allows players to purchase additional chips (up to a limited number of times) when they get broke during a specified period of time, usually, the first three rounds or first few hours. Compare to UNLIMITED REBUY TOURNAMENT.

multiway: Three or more players competing for a pot.

multiway draw: A hand with both straight and flush draw possibilities.

must-move: In a cardroom, a game in which players are forced to move to the main game. This often describes a secondary game at the same limit. "Table 3 is a must-move $20/$40."

nail: 1. Catch a needed card. "I nailed the flush when a five of heart came on the turn." **2.** Get a needed win. **3.** Beat a player. "I nailed his hide tonight." **4.** Achieve a victory. "I nailed it!"

naked flush draw: A hand with four suited cards needing one more to make a flush but having no other possibilities of improving to a winner.

naked straight draw: A hand with four consecutive cards needing one more to make a straight, but having no other possibilities of improving to be a winner.

napkins: Worthless cards.

narrow the field: Cause players to fold by betting or raising, thus creating fewer opponents to compete against for the pot.

natural royal flush: In WILD-CARD POKER, a ROYAL FLUSH, A-K-Q-J-10 in the same suit, made *without* using wild cards.

natural: 1. In WILD-CARD POKER, a card that is not wild. **2.** In wild-card poker, a hand made without wild cards.

needle: Make fun of an opponent either good-naturedly or with the intention of inciting him to get angry and play recklessly.

negative expectation: When a player or a hand is mathematically favored to lose in the long run, as opposed to POSITIVE EXPECTATION.

"Nice hand": "Good hand."

nickel: 1. A $5 chip or bet. **2.** In very large games, a $500 or $5,000 chip or bet.

night shift: Graveyard.

9: The card with nine pips on it and the number 9. A standard deck has four such cards, one in each suit.

nine-handed: 1. A poker game played with nine players or a game that currently has nine players seated. **2.** A pot contested by nine players.

9-perfect: In ace-to-five lowball, the hand 9-4-3-2-A.

nines: A pair of nines.

nit: Tight player who takes no chances, and is thus, very predictable. Even tighter is a *supernit*.

no-brainer: A hand or situation that is so obvious that the proper course of action is clear.

no fold'em: A game in which players typically play to the final round without folding, often found in lower-limit games with less skilled players.

no fold'em hold'em: The hold'em version of NO FOLD'EM.

no gamble in him: Derogatory description of a player who is too tight and won't play speculative or underdog hands.

no-limit: Betting structure in which the maximum bet allowed is limited only by the amount of chips the bettor has on the table.

nonstandard hand: In some private poker variations, card combinations that have value only in the variations played or concocted by the participants but that would normally have no value in standard poker games as played in cardrooms or casinos. For example, a *bobtail straight*, a nonstandard four-straight that sometimes ranks higher than a pair and lower than a four-card flush.

no pair: A poker hand that ranks lower than ONE PAIR, consisting of five unmatched cards not in sequence and of at least two different suits. Also called *high card*.

no-pair: A hand that consists of NO PAIR. "He had a no-pair loser."

no qualifier: 1. In HIGH-LOW POKER, a specific hand that does not meet the low-hand requirement. **2.** In high-low poker, when no players have a qualified low hand and the best high hand wins the entire pot.

no-rebuy tournament: A tournament in which players who lose all their chips are eliminated—they are not allowed to purchase more chips. Opposite of a REBUY TOURNAMENT.

no risk: 1. When nothing further can be lost. **2.** A situation with no down side.

no suits: 1. A board that has cards of different suits. Also see RAINBOW FLOP. **2.** Starting cards of different suits.

not in the hand: A player not actively competing for a pot.

number four: In LOWBALL, the fourth-best hand possible. In DEUCE-TO-SEVEN, it is 7-6-5-4-2 and in ACE-TO-FIVE, the hand 6-5-4-2-A.

number one: In LOWBALL, the best hand possible. In DEUCE-TO-SEVEN, it is 7-5-4-3-2 and in ACE-TO-FIVE, the hand 5-4-3-2-A.

number three: In LOWBALL, the third-best hand possible. In DEUCE-TO-SEVEN, it is 7-6-5-3-2 and in ACE-TO-FIVE, the hand 6-5-3-2-A.

number two: In LOWBALL, the second-best hand possible. In DEUCE-TO-SEVEN, it is 7-6-4-3-2 and in ACE-TO-FIVE, the hand 6-4-3-2-A.

nurse: Carefully guard one's stack in a game by playing conservatively and not putting much at risk on any bet.

nut: 1. The minimum monetary requirements a player needs to earn or to survivor. **2.** The break-even point for a gambler. **3.** The best possible hand given the cards in play. **4.** When referring to a straight or flush, the best possible hand of its type. "The ace gave him the nut flush."

nut flush: The best flush possible, given the cards on board.

nut flush draw: A draw to the NUT FLUSH.

nut high: In HIGH-LOW or high poker, the best high hand possible, given the cards on board.

nut low: In HIGH-LOW or low poker, the best low hand possible, given the cards on board.

nut low draw: In HIGH-LOW or low poker, a draw to the best low hand given the cards on board.

nut-nut: In HIGH-LOW POKER, having the best possible high hand and the best possible low hand given the cards on board.

nuts: The best possible hand given the cards on board; usually expressed as *the nuts*.

nut straight: The best straight possible given the cards on board.

nut straight draw: A draw to the NUT STRAIGHT.

nutted up: 1. A supertight game, one that contains players who bet only very strong hands. **2.** A player holding the NUTS. "He bet out when he got nutted up on the turn."

obvious play: A play that is predictable or should have been predictable.

odd chip: In a SPLIT POT, an extra indivisible chip that remains after all the chips are split evenly.

odds: 1. The mathematical expression showing the percentage chance of an event occurring, typically expressed in numerical format such as 5 to 1 or 3 to 2, with the chances of the event not occurring listed first, and the chances of it occurring, listed second. Odds of 5 to 1 is also expressed as *5 to 1 against,* which means that out of six times, one would expect the event not to occur five times and occur once. **2.** The betting odds established for such situation, that is, what someone booking the situation would pay.

odds against: See ODDS.

off: Short for OFFSUIT. "He had A-Q off against my kings."

office hours: 1. In hold'em, hole cards of 9-5. **2.** The hours a poker player is at the table and pursuing his vocation.

offsuit: 1. Cards of different suits. For example, *K-Q offsuit* means a king and a queen that are not of the same suit. Also, *unsuited.* **2.** A card of a different suit than a potential flush draw. "An offsuit king came on the river."

Oldsmobile: In hold'em, hole cards of 9-8, or in lowball, a 9-8 hand; named for the (now defunct) Oldsmobile 98 car.

Omaha: 1. A high poker game featuring four starting downcards, a FLOP of three shared COMMUNITY CARDS, a fourth community card (the TURN), and then a fifth (the RIVER), with four betting rounds. At the showdown, the final hand must consist of two cards from the player's hand—no more, no less—and three cards from the board (as opposed to HOLD'EM in which any five cards can be used). The best five-card hand wins the pot. Can be played high or HIGH-LOW. **2.** Specifically, the high-only version of the game, and which is sometimes called *Omaha high*.

Omaha 8: OMAHA 8-OR-BETTER.

Omaha 8-or-better: OMAHA played HIGH-LOW with a requirement that the best low hand must have five unpaired cards of 8 or lower to win the low half of the pot or else the best high hand will win the entire pot.

Omaha high: OMAHA played high only.

Omaha high-low 8-or-better: OMAHA 8-OR-BETTER.

one-and-two-chip blind structure: A BLIND structure in which one chip is used for the small blind and two for the big blind, as in a $2/$4 game, which has blinds of $1 and $2. Compare with TWO-AND-FOUR CHIP BLIND STRUCTURE.

one bet: In LIMIT POKER, a bet of one unit, as opposed to *two bets*, in which a bet and a raise are made or owed (or three or four bets). Also, SINGLE BET.

one-bet level: In LIMIT POKER with a two-tier structure, the first and lower level of betting that occurs in the early rounds, as opposed to the TWO-BET LEVEL. For example, in a $5/$10 game, the $5 level of betting. Also, *single bet level.*

one-card draw: In DRAW POKER variations, the exchange of one unwanted card on the draw for a new one.

one-dimensional: In HIGH-LOW poker, a hand that can win either the high or the low end of the pot, but not both, as opposed to TWO DIMENSIONAL.

one direction: In HIGH-LOW poker, a hand that only has strength as a high or low hand.

one-ended straight: A STRAIGHT DRAW involving the cards A-2-3-4 or A-K-Q-J in which only one end of the straight can be filled, in the first case with a 5, in the second, with a king. Compare with INSIDE STRAIGHT and OPEN-ENDED STRAIGHT. Also, *one-sided straight, one-ender.*

one-ender: ONE-ENDED STRAIGHT.

one-eyed jack: J♥ or J♠, named for the one-eye visible on the design.

one-eyed king: K♦, named for the one eye visible on the design.

one-gap: INSIDE STRAIGHT.

one-gapper: INSIDE STRAIGHT.

one on one: HEAD TO HEAD.

one minute: A sixty second time restriction imposed on a player to complete his hand or have it automatically folded. Also, SIXTY SECONDS.

1/1/2: A three blind structure, with the first two blinds of equal size and the third, double the amount, for example, a $1/$1/$2 game or a $5/$5/$10 game. Usually the BUTTON has a blind of $1, the SMALL BLIND is also $1, and the BIG BLIND is $2.

one-outer: A hand that can improve enough to win only by catching one remaining card. For example, if one player has a full house and the other player has 5♦ 6♦ 7♦ 9♦, only a draw of the 8♦ will win the pot for the second player.

one pair: A poker hand containing two cards of the same rank, such as Q-Q or 7-7.

one-sided straight: ONE-ENDED STRAIGHT.

one table satellite: SINGLE-TABLE SATELLITE.

1 to 3: SPREAD-LIMIT POKER played with stakes of $1-$3.

1 to 4: SPREAD-LIMIT POKER played with stakes of $1-$4.

1 to 5: SPREAD-LIMIT POKER played with stakes of $1-$5.

one-way straight: ONE-ENDED STRAIGHT.

online cardroom: An Internet cardroom hosting poker games.

online poker: Poker played on the Internet as opposed to "live" poker, in which players are actually seated together at a physical table. Also, *Internet poker*.

online poker site: ONLINE CARDROOM.

on the board: 1. In a stud or flop game, the face-up cards. **2.** A player who is listed on the waiting BOARD for a seat to become available in a poker game.

on the bubble: In a tournament, the point at which all remaining players will win money except for the next player to get eliminated. For example, when there are 37 players remaining and only 36 places are paid. See BUBBLE.

on the button: The player who occupies the DEALER POSITION and has the dealer BUTTON in front of him.

on the come: Betting on a hand which is an underdog and needs improvement to win, usually referring to a draw to an unmade straight or flush.

on the rail: Busted and out of a game. See RAIL.

on the square: A game or person that is fair and honest. Also, *on the up and up*.

on the up and up: ON THE SQUARE.

on tilt: A player who has lost control of his emotions due to a bad loss or succession of losses and is playing recklessly. The term is borrowed from what happens to a pinball machine when it is shaken too violently and no longer operates properly. Also, *steaming*.

open: 1. Be the first player to make a bet in a round or game.
   2. A game that welcomes all players who wish to participate.
   3. Cards that are dealt FACE UP in any game.

open at both ends: A four-card STRAIGHT DRAW that can be filled on either end, such as 10-J-Q-K, which can be filled with either a 9 or an ace.

open card: A card dealt FACE UP.

open-ended draw: OPEN ENDED STRAIGHT.

open-ended straight: Four consecutive cards to a STRAIGHT (not including an ace, which would make it a ONE-ENDED STRAIGHT) such as 8-9-10-J, such that a card on either end will make a straight, as opposed to an INSIDE or ONE-ENDED STRAIGHT. Also, *eight-way straight, double-ended straight, open-ended draw, outside draw*.

open-ender: OPEN ENDED STRAIGHT.

opener: The player making the first wager in a betting round or the wager itself.

openers: A hand of sufficient strength to legally open the betting in a game that requires such, or the specific cards that fulfill the requirement. For example, in JACKS OR BETTER, a hand of at least jacks is required to open the betting, and either the hand or just those two jacks are called *openers*. Also *qualifier*.

open game: A poker game open to all players, as opposed to a PRIVATE GAME, which is open to invited guests only.

opening bet: The first bet made in a betting round.

opening requirements: 1. A minimum hand value established in a game that requires OPENERS, such as JACKS OR BETTER, where a hand of two jacks or higher is required for the opening bet.
2. A player's strategy guidelines for when he will initiate betting, that is, the minimum holding he needs to enter a pot.

open on both ends: OPEN AT BOTH ENDS.

open pair: In a stud game, two cards of the same rank, such as 9-9 (a pair), that are exposed on a board.

open poker: STUD POKER.

open seat: 1. An available seat at a table for a new player. **2.** SEAT OPEN.

"Open seat on...": SEAT OPEN ON.

open the betting: Make the first bet in a betting round.

open up: Play more hands than previously; generally applied to a player who is playing tight and changes gears to a more loose style. See CHANGE GEARS.

option: An option held by the big blind on the preflop when no raises have preceded his position, to simply call and end the betting in the round, or to put in a raise.

"option?": A query by the dealer asking the big blind if he wishes to call and end the betting in the round, or to put in a raise on the preflop.

ORAC: A poker-playing computer program developed by well-known poker author Mike "The Mad Genius" Caro; ORAC is his name spelled backwards.

oral bet: A bet that is verbally announced (and binding in public cardrooms), regardless of whether the specified number of chips, if any, are actually placed into the pot. Also, *verbal bet*, *mouth bet*.

original hand: In DRAW POKER, the initial five cards dealt.

out: 1. A card that will improve a player's hand enough to win the pot, often expressed in the plural. "On the river, Johnny had twelve outs, his nine flush cards and three aces that would give him a winning pair." See OUTS. **2.** A player who is not involved in a pot or has folded. "I'm out of this hand." **3.** Not receiving cards. "Deal me out this hand."

outdraw: Receive more favorable cards than an opponent, enough to win.

outflop: Make a better hand on the FLOP than an opponent.

out of line: 1. Betting aggressively with weak hands, hoping to force opponents out of the pot; bluffing. **2.** A player whose behavior is offensive or unacceptable.

out-of-line play: A bluff.

out of position: 1. Being in the disadvantageous POSITION of acting before opponents. **2.** In early position, with one or more active players after.

out of turn: Acting on a hand before one is supposed to, which is a breath of poker etiquette, as opposed to IN TURN.

out on a limb: Making a risky play or being in a risky situation.

outplay: On a specific hand or overall, play at a superior skill level than one or more opponents.

outs: Cards that will improve a hand that is behind enough to win a pot. For example, a hand of 7-7-9-9-K has four outs against a completed straight, the two remaining sevens and nines, which will make a winning full house, while a player who needs to complete a four card flush draw to win, has nine outs, the remaining suited cards in the deck.

outside draw: Open-ended straight.

outside gambler: Road gambler.

outside wrap: In Omaha, a straight draw that combines with the highest board cards, for example holding Q-J-8-2 with a board of 10-9-2.

over: The connecting term in the naming of a two pair hand, as in *kings over deuces*, indicating that the first pair mentioned, kings, in this example, is the higher pair, and the second, deuces, is the lower pair.

◆

overaggressive: A player who bets and raises too much.

overbet: 1. In NO-LIMIT poker, bet more than a standard amount in a given situation. **2.** In POT-LIMIT, bet more than the amount of the current size of the pot (which is not permitted), with the OVERS, the extra chips, being returned.

overbet the pot: 1. In POT-LIMIT, bet more than the size of the pot. **2.** In NO-LIMIT poker, bet more than what seems a reasonable amount, usually more than the size of the pot.

overcall: 1. Call a bet after another player has already called. "Jackie bet $5, Rose-Marie called, and Angie overcalled." **2.** At the showdown, announce a hand as being superior to what is actually held. Compare with MISCALL.

overcard: A HOLE CARD higher in rank than any board card. For example, if a player holds A-10 and the flop is K-J-6, the ace is an overcard.

overchip: OVERSIZED CHIP.

overfull: In flop games, a full house in which the three of a kind portion combines with the highest-ranking board card for a higher-ranking full house than one that combines with a lesser-ranking board card. For example, in hold'em, if the board is J-7-3-10-J, a player holding J-10 has an *overfull* compared to someone holding 7-7, which is called an UNDERFULL.

overhead: 1. The average fixed costs of playing poker, which in a cardroom or Internet setting, is the estimated amount of RAKE a player must pay as commission on every hand or every hour of play. **2.** The overall expenses a professional must meet while he pursues a living in poker.

overpair: In hold'em and Omaha, a pocket pair that is larger than any open card on the board. For example, Q-Q on a flop of J-10-6. Compare with UNDERPAIR.

overs: 1. A bet that is higher than the permissible amount, with the *overs* part of the bet, the extra chips, to be returned to the player. **2.** A special circumstance in which two or more players agree to raise the stakes to a certain limit at any point in a hand when play involves only them. For example, in a $4/$8 game, two or more players might agree to *play overs* for stakes of $10/$20. At whatever point in a hand non-overs players all fold, the stakes jump from $4/$8 to $10/$20.

overs button: A button used in games in which players, by prearranged agreement, are playing OVERS.

overset: TOP SET.

oversize bet: A bet that is larger than the situation warrants.

oversized chip: A chip, put into a pot, of greater value than what is required. For example, a player puts a $100 chip in for a $50 blind (and thus, needs it changed) or puts in a $1,000 chip when it is his turn to call a $100 bet. Also, *overchip*.

oversize raise: A raise of more than typical size.

over the top: See COME OVER THE TOP.

pack of cards: See DECK.

paint: 1. Jack, queen, or king in any suit—cards that are "painted." Also *picture card*, *court card*, *face card*. **2.** Illegal markings put on a card by a cheat.

painted: In LOW POKER, having caught a face card. "I lost when I painted on the end."

paired: A card that matches another card of the same rank to form a pair. "On fourth street, the king paired his door card, giving him two pair, kings and sixes."

paired board: In hold'em and Omaha, a board containing a pair, such as Q-4-4.

palmed card: A card concealed in the palm of a hand.

paper deck: A pack of cards that is made of paper (rather than the more durable and higher quality plastic deck).

paper hanger: An individual who writes checks he can't cover, that is, "rubber" or bad checks.

partner: 1. A player who shares a bankroll, and attendant wins and losses, with another individual or group. **2.** A confederate in a scam or cheating operation.

"Pasadena": Fold.

pass: Decline to bet; CHECK; sometimes, FOLD.

pass and out: A game in which no checking is allowed on the first round; a player either bets or folds. This is the usual case in BLIND GAMES.

passed pot: In draw poker, usually applying to JACKS OR BETTER, when no player has opened the betting in a round and the cards are redealt for a new game.

passive: 1. A player who rarely raises. **2.** A game that has little or no raising, and thus relatively small pots.

passive game: A game with little or no raising, as opposed to an ACTION GAME.

pass the trash: See ANACONDA.

pat: In DRAW games, a hand to which no cards are drawn. "I'm pat."

pat hand: In DRAW games, a hand to which no cards are drawn.

pay off: 1. Call bets with cards thought to be inferior in the hopes that the hand improves into a winner or that the opponent's hand is weaker than expected. **2.** Call with what appears to be a losing hand because the caller suspects that the opponent is bluffing. Also, *keep someone honest*. **3.** Call for the purpose of seeing an opponent's cards. **4:** Induce an opponent into calling or betting on a hand in which he is already beat

payoff: Potential or actual winnings.

payout: 1. Amount won or to be won. **2.** In a tournament, the prize money distributed to the winners.

pay someone off: PAY OFF.

peddle the nuts: SELL THE NUTS.

peek: 1. Quickly look at one's cards. **2.** Intentionally look at other players' concealed cards or cards being dealt or yet to be dealt.

pelican: A sophisticated player who feeds off the inferior players (the FISH); that is, he wins their money.

penny-ante game: 1. A game played for pennies. **2.** A game played for very small stakes.

perfect: In ACE-TO-FIVE, the best possible four-card low along with a higher low card. For example, an *8-perfect*, 8-4-3-2-A.

perfect catch: Drawing of the best possible card.

perfect low: In LOWBALL or HIGH-LOW, the best possible low hand. In ACE-TO-FIVE, A-2-3-4-5, and in DEUCE-TO-SEVEN, 2-3-4-5-7. Often called a WHEEL.

perfect-perfect: RUNNER-RUNNER.

perfects: In LOWBALL or HIGH-LOW, premium low cards, A, 2, 3, 4 or 5.

pick off: 1. Call a bluffer's bet, usually on the end, and win.
2. Raise a bluffer's bet with a rebluff and win when he folds.

pick up: 1. Win a pot, usually with a bet or raise that forces out opponents. **2.** Catch a card that improves or makes a hand.

pick up a hand: 1. Be dealt strong starting cards. **2.** Play a hand for someone. "Will you pick up a hand for me while I go to the bathroom?"

pick up a pot: Win a hand, particularly when opponents fold.

picture card: Paint.

piece: Stake a player and receive a percentage of his winnings. "I've got a piece of Mac in the main event."

piece of cheese: Lousy hand. "Throw that piece of cheese in the muck."

pigeon: Bad player.

pineapple: A variation of hold'em in which players start with three cards instead of two, then discard one of them before the flop.

pink eye: Pink or red tinted contact lenses worn by a cheater to identify marked cards.

◆

pip: The suit symbols on a card traditionally signifying its rank. For example, the 6♦ has six diamond-shaped pips on its face side. Also, *spot*.

plastic deck: A pack of cards that is made of plastic (more durable and of higher quality than a paper deck).

play: 1. Actively participate in a hand or game. **2.** A bluff or fancy move, often part of the term *make a play*. **3.** Description of action. "The game had plenty of play." **4.** The ability to maneuver in a tournament or a blind structure in which skill has a greater influence than luck. "The main event has plenty of play. Players start with $10,000 in chips and the levels are ninety minutes."

playable: A hand that has enough merit to warrant betting or calling.

play a rush: Play more hands during a winning streak in the belief that winning begets winning.

play back: Raise or reraise an opponent's bet or raise.

play behind: 1. When a player will cover bets that are in excess of the amount of money that he has on the table, as opposed to TABLE STAKES. **2.** Being in LATE POSITION relative to other players competing for a pot.

play by the book: Follow commonly accepted principles of strategy without getting fancy or deviating.

player: 1. A participant in a game or in a pot. **2.** An individual who is skillful in a game. "Jones is a player." **3.** A regular participant who is knowledgeable about the milieu of the game.

Player: The gambling lifestyle magazine *Avery Cardoza's Player*.

play fast: Bet aggressively.

play (it) straight: Bet or raise in the expected manner, that is, not use tricky or fancy plays.

"Plays as it lays": A declaration that the chip amount in front of a player is the actual amount of the bet (and not a lesser amount). For example, if a bet of $100 is due, and a player tosses in a $500 chip while stating quietly that he is raising, the dealer may make this announcement to players on the other side of the table who may not have heard what the bettor said to indicate that this is not a call, but a raise. See OVERSIZED CHIP.

play the board: In hold'em, use all five cards from the board as one's best hand.

play the percentages: Make plays and decisions that, mathematically, are the most likely to show a long-term profit.

play the player: Make strategic decisions based on the merits or weaknesses of an opponent as opposed to his cards or the situation.

play with: Bet or raise or call an opponent's bets or raises and stay ACTIVE in a pot.

p.m.: SWING SHIFT.

pocket: In flop and stud games, the face-down cards held individually by each player. "When Vinny reraised, we knew he had either pocket kings or pocket aces."

pocket aces: A pair of aces as one's HOLE CARDS. In hold'em, the best possible starting cards.

pocket cards: The initial cards a player is dealt; in hold'em (two cards) and Omaha (four cards). In stud games, the facedown cards held individually by each player. Also HOLE CARDS, STARTING CARDS.

pocket cowboys: A pair of kings as one's HOLE CARDS. In hold'em, the second-best possible starting cards.

pocket pair: A PAIR as one's HOLE CARDS.

pocket rockets: POCKET ACES.

points: A percentage invested or received in another player's winnings or a company's earnings, with each point representing one percent.

POKER TALK

poker: A card game of many varieties, featuring one or more betting rounds, and in which players win by either having the highest ranking hand or by forcing out all opponents through heavy betting such that they win the hand by default before the last round of play.

poker chip: A CHIP used as currency in poker games.

poker face: A stone-like and unreadable facial expression that gives away no clues as to the strength of the cards a player is holding.

poker hand: 1. A player's best five cards. **2.** Any of the standard and valid poker rankings from no pair up to a royal flush.

poker player: An individual who plays the game of poker.

poker room: A CARDROOM, CASINO, or physical room in which poker is played.

poker table: 1. A table specifically built for the game of poker around which players gather, the cards are dealt, and all the poker action takes place. **2.** Any table on which poker is played or where players are playing poker.

"Pony up": 1. ANTE UP. **2.** Place money into the pot to meet a bet or raise that is due.

pool: The British term for POT.

pop: RAISE.

pop it: RAISE.

position: 1. A player's relative order of acting compared to opponents, particularly with respect to the number of players acting after his turn. **2.** Specifically good position, that is later and better than opponents. "When you're on the button, you have position and can open with more hands."

positional bluff: Using the leverage of late POSITION, a bet or raise made with inferior cards for the purpose of inducing opponents to fold.

position bet: A bet made based on having good POSITION, that is, acting later than opponents, rather than on the absolute strength of the hand.

positive expectation: A player or a hand that is mathematically favored to win in the long run, as opposed to NEGATIVE EXPECTATION.

post: 1. Put up a blind. *The first two players to the left of the button post blinds in hold'em.* **2.** Place a missing blind bet. **3.** Make a bet.

post-oak bluff: When the pot is large in a no-limit or pot-limit game, a small bet made with a weak hand, with the intention of having opponents fold and give up the pot.

pot: The total of all bets placed in the center of the table by players during a poker hand and collected by the winner or winners of that hand.

pot-committed: To bet so much of one's stack, usually around half or more of one's chips, that in effect, a bettor has decided to commit all his chips to the pot if he is raised.

"Pot is right": A statement, usually by the dealer, verifying that the amount in the pot is correct.

pot-limit: A betting structure in which the maximum bet allowed is limited by the current size of the pot. The more money that goes into the pot, the larger the bets that are allowed. For example, if the pot is $25, a player may bet $25, and the next player can either call the $25 bet, raise it $50 (the minimum raise), or raise $75 (the size of the pot including his $25 call). The upper betting limit increases every time a bet is made until a hand is over, when the betting limits drop down to the starting amounts for the game.

pot odds: The amount of money in the pot compared to the cost of a bet. For example if $50 is in the pot, and a player needs to call a bet of $10 to play, he is getting pot odds of 5 to 1. Compare with IMPLIED ODDS.

pot-stuck: Having invested so much money into a pot that a player feels he is unable to fold against a bet or raise and must call, even though he feels he is getting the worst of it.

pound: Bet and raise aggressively.

power: A player who is leading the betting and raising in a hand. In games, you may hear players who are due to act before a player who raised on previous rounds say, "Check to the power," giving respect to their aggressive opponent and letting him make the first move in the current round.

PPT: PROFESSIONAL POKER TOUR.

preflop: In hold'em, Omaha, and other flop variations, the action that occurs after players receive their starting cards and before the three-card FLOP is dealt.

premium: 1. BONUS. **2.** Pertaining to a PREMIUM HAND.

premium cards: 1. PREMIUM HAND. **2.** In hold'em, in certain instances, referring to the highest two cards, the ace or king. "I was low-stacked and going to move all in with any premium cards."

premium hand: One in a group of the best starting hands in a poker game.

preselect button: EARLY ACTION BUTTON.

press: 1. Bet more aggressively than is prudent, perhaps due to feeling pressure. **2.** Double one's bets.

price: 1. The cost of playing a hand. **2.** The risk versus the reward on any given play or situation. "He got a good price on that hand and decided to call."

primary cards: The cards a player holds that give him the best chance to win the pot, although he also has SECONDARY CARDS. For example, in Omaha high-low, a player holds A♠-K♠-Q♥-8♣ with a flop of Q♥-6♠-3♠. His *primary cards* are A♠-K♠, which give him a nut flush draw and top pair, while his *secondary cards* are A♠-8♣, because he could make an EMERGENCY LOW, which, while not very good, might win half the pot.

private game: A poker game restricted to invited members or held in a noncommercial poker room. Opposite of PUBLIC GAME. When played in a private home, known as a HOME GAME.

prize pool: In a tournament, the total amount of money to be awarded to the top finishers.

producer: An inferior player with a large bankroll, one who feeds the winning purses of superior players. Also, any of the following with a large bankroll: CUSTOMER, FISH, LIVE ONE, PIGEON, PROVIDER.

professional: PROFESSIONAL POKER PLAYER.

professional poker player: One who makes his living playing poker.

Professional Poker Tour: An invitation-only freeroll tour comprised of many of the world's best tournament players and run by the World Poker Tour. Also, *PPT*.

progressive poker: A game in which the bets increase after no one has bet the previous pot.

prop: 1. PROPOSITION BET. **2.** PROPOSITION PLAYER.

prop bet: PROPOSITION BET.

proposition bet: 1. A wager made by poker players on a particular event occurring during a game, one that has no relation to poker skills. For example, in hold'em, players may make a proposition bet that three suited cards come on the flop. **2.** A side bet that might be made by players in contention for a pot, usually at less than true odds, of a hand winning under certain circumstance.

proposition player: 1. A cardroom employee who starts poker games and fills in a seat at short-handed tables. Although he works for the cardroom, he plays with his own money, as opposed to a SHILL. Also *prop, public relations player*. **2.** A player who makes or likes to make PROPOSITION BETS.

protect a hand: 1. Carefully cover one's cards when looking so that opponents cannot read their values. **2.** Place a chip or other small token over one's cards so that the dealer doesn't mistakenly remove them (causing the hand to be folded) or so that no discards inadvertently mix with the player's cards (which would foul the hand). **3.** Bet or raise with a leading but vulnerable hand so that opponents have to pay a steep price to go for a lucky draw, in an attempt to cause speculative hands to fold. "He raised on fifth street to protect his set."

public game: A game open to all legal players, played in a cardroom or casino. Opposite of PRIVATE GAME.

public relations player: PROPOSITION PLAYER.

pull: JUICE, definition 1.

pull it in: When there is a raise, pull all players' bets into the pot so that the extra chips of the raise can clearly be identified as the amount that opponents must match to stay active in a pot. Also, *bring it in*.

pump the pot: Build up the pot by betting and raising aggressively.

punters: A British term for bettors.

push: 1. A tie or split pot, a term borrowed from other casino games, such as blackjack. **2.** Change of dealers. "There hasn't been a push in ninety minutes; this is ridiculous." **3.** Bet or raise at a player, forcing him to react. **4.** Bet and raise too aggressively. "Johnson was pushing hard and I broke him when I turned the nut flush."

push around: Bully with aggressive betting and raising to force conservative players out of the pot or into big pot situations they want to avoid.

push through: Change dealers. "We will push through, table by table, after the break."

put a play on: Bluff.

put a player on a hand: 1. Deduce an opponent's hand by his betting and playing actions. **2.** Assume that a player has a good hand. "When he kept raising, I put him on a hand and folded." In this sense, also GIVE CREDIT TO.

put someone in a game: Bankroll a player in return for a percentage of the profits. Also, STAKE.

put the brakes on: Discontinue aggressive betting and raising and play passively.

POKER TALK

◆

put the clock on: A time limit imposed on a player who takes an excessively long time to make a decision, such that if he doesn't act within the limit (of usually one minute), his hand is automatically folded. Can be initiated by the request of any player.

Q: Symbol used in written text for a queen in any suit.

quadruple through: Increase a bankroll by a multiple of four on a single hand or in a session.

quads: Four of a kind.

qualifier: 1. In high-low poker variations, the requirements that a low hand must meet to be eligible to win the low end of the pot. For example, in Omaha or stud 8-or-better, the highest card in the low hand must be no higher than an 8 (and that hand must consist of five unpaired cards), or the hand cannot qualify for the low. **2.** In high poker variations, a hand that must be of sufficient strength to legally open betting, for example, having a hand of at least jacks in jacks or better. Also, openers.

qualify: 1. In HIGH-LOW poker variations, be eligible to win the low half of a pot. **2.** In HIGH poker variations that have a QUALIFIER requirement, have a hand that is eligible to open.

quality hand: A hand that is of reasonable strength to win or to improve to win a pot.

quarter: 1. One fourth of a pot. **2.** $25 or a $25 chip (which is also sometimes called a GREEN CHIP). **3.** In very high-limit games, $25,000 or a $25,000 chip.

quartered: In a HIGH-LOW game, having split either the low or high end of a pot such that only one-fourth of the chips are won.

queen: The card with a stylized image of a queen on it and the letter Q, of which a deck contains four, one in each suit.

queens: A pair of queens.

quit: 1. Stop play. **2.** Leave a game.

quitting time: 1. A prearranged time at which players agree that a game will stop. **2.** In a cardroom, closing time, at which point the house stops dealing and the game is over.

rabbit hunting: Dealing out undealt cards in games so that players can see the hands they would have made, a practice typically disallowed or discouraged in cardrooms.

race off: In a tournament, when all the smaller denomination chips are COLORED UP to the next highest denomination so that the smaller chips will no longer be in play, with the odd leftover chips, colored-up and awarded to players dealt the highest cards, with a one chip per player maximum.

rack: 1. A plastic tray made to hold 100 chips, five equal stacks of twenty per row. **2.** The tray used by a house dealer to hold chips, extra cards, cash, and other necessities of the job. **3.** Put chips into a rack. "Rack 'em up; it's time to move."

rag: A worthless card not thought to help anyone; BRICK.

ragged: In hold'em and Omaha, a board without premium cards and with no good straight or flush possibilities, such as J-8-2 of three different suits.

rail: 1. In a cardroom, a barrier that separates onlookers from players. **2.** Figuratively, a place where onlookers watch. **3.** Where a player goes, literally or figuratively, when he busts out of a game. "I put my last $100 in the pot with a flush, my opponent showed me a full house, and I was on the rail."

railbird: Someone who watches poker from the RAIL, due either to being knocked out of a game, because he cannot afford to play, or simply because he is a spectator.

railroad bible: A deck of cards.

rainbow: Cards of different suits. "The flop came 10-J-K rainbow."

rainbow flop: A flop of three different suits.

raise: 1. A wager that increases the size of a current bet such that opponents, including the original bettor, must put additional money into the pot to stay active in a hand. **2.** The actual chips or money that constitute this action. **3.** In a tournament or a game, an increase of the betting limits. **4.** Make a raise.

POKER TALK

raised pot: A pot that has already had a RAISE in the current or previous rounds of betting, often meaning a raise that was made on the first round of betting.

raise on the come: RAISE with a hand that is not yet formed (usually a draw to a straight or flush) and that needs at least one card to improve to a winner.

raiser: A player who RAISES or has raised in the hand.

raising hand: A hand that is good enough to RAISE with.

rake: The amount of money taken out of a pot by the house as its fee for running a game. Also, *table charge, bite, vigorish, juice.*

ram and jam: Play aggressively, betting and raising often.

rammer-jammer: A player who gives lots of ACTION, betting and raising frequently.

rammin' and jammin': Betting and raising aggressively, often used to describe a particular game.

rank: The value or denomination of a card, for example, a 2 or a jack. Rank does not refer to the suit.

rank of cards: The order of strength of individual cards. In high games, from strongest to weakest, they are A-K-Q-J-10-9-8-7-6-5-4-3-2; in ACE-TO-FIVE low games, A-2-3-4-5-6-7-8-9-10-J-Q-K (the king being the highest and thus worst card); in DEUCE-TO-SEVEN low games, from strongest to weakest, 2-3-4-5-6-7-8-9-10-J-Q-K-A (the ace being the highest and thus worst card).

rank of hands: The order of combinations that make up poker hands. From best to worst in standard high poker: royal flush, straight flush, four of a kind, full house, flush, straight, three of a kind, two pair, pair, high card (ace highest, king next highest, and so on down).

rap pat: In draw poker, draw no additional cards or the physical act of knocking on the table to indicate such.

Raquel Welsh: In hold'em, hole cards of 3-8, named after the famous actress's supposed bust size.

rathole: Remove chips from play during a game and place in one's pocket.

razz: Seven-card stud played for low.

read: 1. Be able to deduce an opponent's hand given the cards seen, his position, and his betting. Also, *put a player on a hand.* **2.** Figure out the possible hands that could be made given the cards seen. **3.** See READ THE BOARD.

read an opponent: READ, definition 1.

read the board: In hold'em and Omaha, understand the possible hands that can be formed in combination with the community cards face up on the table.

real poker: Poker played in any form, especially when money is put at risk.

real world poker: Poker played with players physically present at the same table, as opposed to ONLINE POKER. Also *face-to-face poker, live poker.*

rebuy: The purchase of more chips. Often, specifically such purchase in a REBUY TOURNAMENT.

rebuy period: In a rebuy tournament, the period of time—usually the first three rounds—during which players can purchase additional chips if they fall below a specified total.

rebuy tournament: A tournament that allows players to buy more chips when they lose all their current ones, an option usually restricted to the first three levels of play or sometimes to an initial specified period, say, one hour. Generally rebuys are restricted to some maximum number (often one), with the exception of an UNLIMITED REBUY TOURNAMENT.

recall: A poker player's ability to remember how an opponent or class of opponents played a type of hand or situation in the past.

red: 1. A hand or board consisting of only red cards—hearts and diamonds. "He held red aces, which did him no good when the flop came up three spades." **2.** A $5 chip (typically red in color), also called a REDBIRD.

redbird: A red chip, usually worth $5.

red chip: A $5 chip (which is typically red in color).

red-chip game: A modest-sized poker game, one played with red ($5) chips, the standard color in most casinos.

redraw: 1. A random reassignment of tables and seats to remaining players after a tournament has started. **2.** After an opponent gets a lucky card to go ahead, retake the lead with one's own lucky card. **3.** In TRIPLE DRAW and other games with more than one draw, exchange cards an additional time.

regular: A player who is a frequent participant in a game.

related cards: Cards that form straight and flush possibilities.

release a hand: Fold, particularly a good hand.

represent: Bet or raise on cards that appear to indicate a particular hand or type of hand but not actually have that hand. For example, to bet out on a board of four diamonds, as if a flush were held, but not actually hold one.

reraise: Raise a raise, that is, call an opponent's increased bet and commit even more chips to the pot.

---

respect: 1. Assume a player's bet represents strength, that is, a legitimate hand, as opposed to being a bluff. **2.** Give credit to a player's skills or reputation and show the proper deference to his play.

return: The amount of winnings a player makes or expects to make from an investment in a poker game or tournament.

reverse tell: A deliberate mannerism intended specifically to fool an opponent into believing that the opposite type of hand is held.

ride along: 1. Play another round without cost because no bets were made—there were only checks. **2.** Play another round at minimal cost, that is for only the price of a call of one bet or a small bet.

right price: 1. A bet that has good value because the amount in the pot compared to the amount of the bet—THE POT ODDS—justifies it. **2.** Getting good pot odds on a bet or raise.

ringer: A player who pretends to be an amateur but is actually an expert player.

ring game: 1. A CASH GAME with a full table of players, usually seven or more, as opposed to a SHORT GAME, generally one played with six or fewer players. **2.** A cash game specifically as opposed to a tournament game.

risk: Money, chips, or assets wagered and subject to losses.

river: 1. In hold'em and Omaha, the fifth and last community card dealt or its betting round (or both considered together). **2.** In stud games, the last card each player receives or its betting round (or both considered together). Also, END.

river card: RIVER.

riverboat gambler: 1. A professional player who plies his trade on riverboats, usually referring to the players who frequented the Mississippi River paddleboats and steamers in the 1800s. **2.** Dishonest player, a meaning that came from the prevalence of cheats during the heyday of riverboats in the U.S. in the 19th century.

rivered: Having made a hand or received a card on the river, as in *he rivered a jack* or *rivered a set*.

road gambler: A gambler who travels extensively to find and play in games.

rock: 1. A tight player, one who bets only with premium hands, that is, infrequently. **2.** BRICK. "On the turn, he folded when a rock landed and J.J. bet into the pot."

rock garden: A game full of tight players.

rock of all ages: A player who only bets with premium cards and thus, rarely is involved a pot.

roll: 1. Winning streak. **2.** Reveal one's cards at the showdown.

rolled-up: In seven-card stud, three of a kind in the first three cards.

roll your own: Stud variation in which players choose which one of their downcards to reveal on board as their face up or DOOR CARD.

rough: A lowball hand with relatively weak supporting cards, for example, 8-7-6-5-3 is a *rough 8,* as opposed to a *smooth 8*, such as 8-5-3-2-A.

round: 1. In a tournament, a fixed period of play that ends with increased blinds or antes or both. Also *level*. **2.** One complete turn of hands around a table, one per player. "They alternated one round of stud with one round of triple draw." **3.** The complete cycle of checks, bets, folds, and raises occurring after each new card or cards are dealt. **4.** Drinks bought for every player at the table or in a cardroom, a term borrowed from social drinking. "I'd like to buy a round for the table."

rounder: Skilled or professional poker player who plays regularly.

***Rounders*:** A movie about poker players, starring Matt Damon and Edward Norton.

round of betting: A betting turn around a table in which all active players have had a chance to act on their hands.

royal: ROYAL FLUSH.

royal flush: The poker hand consisting of 10-J-Q-K-A of the same suit, the highest-ranking hand in standard poker without wild cards. Sometimes simply called a *royal*. A♠ K♠ Q♠ J♠ 10♠ is a royal flush in spades or a spade royal flush.

royalty: Bonus.

rug joint: An old expression for a cardroom with high-quality décor. Compare to SAWDUST JOINT.

rules: HOUSE RULES.

rules of the game: HOUSE RULES.

run: **1.** A consecutive sequence of cards. **2.** A consecutive sequence or preponderance of events, such as a run of good or bad luck; a STREAK. "I had a good run for a week." **3.** To have a run. "Big J was running hot; he must have won five pots in a row."

run all over: RUN OVER.

rundown: In Omaha, four connecting cards in a player's starting hand. For example, 5-6-7-8 as the starting cards.

"Run 'em": Said by the last player in a betting round, when no bets have been made, to let the dealer know he too has checked and that another round of cards can be dealt.

run it twice: Deal cards a second time using the same starting cards with players (usually two) agreeing to play the hand out two times drawing fresh cards for each hand with half the pot being allocated to the winner of each deal. For example, one river card would be dealt with half the pot awarded to the winner, and then another river card with the remaining half of the pot awarded to the winner based on this new card. Players can agree to run it twice earlier than the river, and can even agree to *run it three times*.

run one: Bluff.

run over: Put pressure on a player or a game by aggressively betting and raising. Also, RUN ALL OVER.

runner: 1. A card that improves a longshot hand into a strong hand, typically used as part of the expression *runner-runner*, in which, generally, a three-card flush or straight draw turns into a completed hand by catching successive good cards on the last two streets. **2.** British term for a player. "Roland edged out 800 runners to win the tournament."

runner-runner: The catching of needed cards on the last two streets to turn a big underdog hand into a winner, usually referring to the filling of a three card straight or flush draw. Also, *perfect-perfect*.

runner-runner-runner: In seven-card stud, catch needed cards in succession on the last three streets to turn an unexpected longshot hand into a winner. The situation also occurs in flop games when the three-card flop is counted as one of the "runners," along with the turn and the river.

running bad: On a losing streak.

running good: On a winning streak.

running pair: Two exposed cards of equal rank that are dealt consecutively either to an individual player in a stud game, or on the board in a flop game.

run through: DOUBLE THROUGH.

rush: 1. A winning streak. 2. Winning a lot of hands or more than the expected share of times in a short period of time.

s: 1. Symbol for spades in written text. 8s is the 8♠. **2.** Symbol for suited in written text, that is, cards of the same suit. *KJs* means K-J suited.

sandbag: To check and then raise, essentially trapping an opponent. The term is often used in an uncomplimentary fashion.

sandwiched: WHIPSAWED.

satellite: SATELLITE TOURNAMENT.

satellite tournament: A one-, sometimes two- or three-, table tournament in which the winner gains entry into a larger-buy-in tournament for a fraction of the cost. For example, $10,000 buy-in tournaments often feature $1,000 satellites preceding the event. Sometimes, a second- and third-place cash prize is awarded as well. With more than a few tables, it becomes a SUPERSATELLITE. With one table, also *single table satellite, one table satellite.*

save: In a tournament, an agreement between players at a final table to divide some portion of the prize money before the final outcome as a way of reducing their risk of losing. Also, DEAL.

sawdust joint: An old down-home type of cardroom or casino of simple décor that caters to a more "local" and lower-income patronage than a RUG JOINT.

say: A player's turn to act. "Your say, podner; whaddaya wanna do?"

SB: SMALL BLIND; used in written text and online cardroom CHAT.

scare card: In flop and stud games, a card dealt on board that presents the possibility of a bigger hand for an opponent. For example, in hold'em, if a player has pocket kings, an ace appearing on the flop would be a scare card because it represents a potentially bigger pair than the king, or similarly; the appearance of a third or fourth suited card on board is a scare card for a player holding a straight.

scared money: Money or chips that a player is afraid to lose, causing him to play so conservatively that he is easily intimidated and bluffed.

scary flop: A three-card flop with combinations that represent possible bigger hands for opponents, for example, in hold'em when a player holds a pair and three cards of one suit appear on the board, forming a possible flush for opponents.

schoolboy draw: A foolish play, one with unfavorable odds (a move that an unlearned schoolboy might make).

scoop: In a HIGH-LOW game, win both the high and low ends of a pot.

scooped pot: In a HIGH-LOW game, when the entire pot is won by a player, usually when he has both the best high and the best low, but also due to having the best high hand in a pot in which there is no qualified (see QUALIFIER) low.

scramble: Randomly mix the cards on the table. Also, *wash.*

seat: 1. An opening in a poker game. "We have a seat available."
2. The position of a player relative to where the dealer sits, with seat one being immediately to the dealers left, seat two being to that player's left, and so on clockwise around the table. **3.** The actual chair on which a player sits. "Elmore liked to put two cushions on his seat so that he sat taller than the other players."
4. An entry place in a tournament. "Didier made it into the top eight places in the satellite and won a seat in the big event."

seat charge: TIME, definition 2.

"Seat open": An announcement by a dealer that a player has left a table in a cash game and a seat has become available; a similar announcement in a tournaments that a player has busted out. "Seat open on seven" (or whatever table has a seat available) is a common call heard in cardrooms or during tournaments. Also, *open seat*.

"Seat open on..." In a tournament or cash game, an announcement that a player has busted out or left and a seat is available at that table.

seat position: A player's SEAT relative to the dealer, which has no bearing on order of play. This is not to be confused with POSITION, a player's seat relative to the dealer BUTTON.

secondary cards: See BACKUP DRAW and PRIMARY CARDS.

secondary draw: BACKUP DRAW.

second best: An ironic term for a hand that is next best to the winner, that is, a loser.

second draw: In TRIPLE DRAW, the second exchange of unwanted cards for new ones.

second nuts: The second-best possible hand given the cards on board. Also see NUTS.

second pair: In flop games, a pair formed by combining a pocket card with the second-highest board card.

security card: CUT CARD.

see: 1. CALL. "I'll see that $20." **2.** In proposition betting, recognize and announce that a winning combination has occurred, thereby making it a valid and winning wager, as opposed to *sleeping a bet*, that is, not noticing the winning combination, and thus forfeiting the payoff.

see a bet: CALL.

see a card: CALL a bet or raise so that another card can be seen.

see the flop: In hold'em and Omaha, call a bet or raise so that the flop can be seen. "Frankie called Joe's raise to see the flop."

see where a player is at: Make a bet for the purpose of seeing how an opponent responds (fold, call, or raise), thus providing valuable information about his hand strength.

sell a hand: In pot-limit, no-limit, and spread-limit games, bet less than a standard amount with the probable best hand, hoping to induce opponents to call.

sell the nuts: Given the cards on board, make a small bet with the very best hand possible to induce opponents to call or raise in a situation they will likely lose.

semibluff: Bet or raise with a hand that is perceived to be second-best or worse but has two ways to win, either by forcing opponents out, or if that fails, by improving to a winner with a fortuitous draw. For example, in hold'em, raising to force out opponents with a hand of 8♥ 7♥ on a board of Q♥ K♥ 6♠, a hand that will likely lose if called, but which could win if another heart is dealt.

sequential declaration: CONSECUTIVE DECLARATION.

session: A period of time that a player gambles, marked by a starting and finishing time.

session bankroll: The amount of money a player sets aside for a gambling outing.

set: THREE OF A KIND.

set over set: A hand in which a three of a kind hand beats out a lesser three of a kind hand.

set someone in: Bet an equal or greater number of chips than an opponent has, causing him to commit all his chips to call the bet.

settle up: At the end of a poker game or at the conclusion of a bet, for players to resolve their debts and winnings with one another.

setup: In cardrooms, either a fresh deck of cards or two decks of cards, each of a different color. When a new deck is needed, you may hear a dealer call out, "Setup on five," indicating that new cards are needed on table five.

set up: 1. Prepare a trap for an opponent. **2.** Prepare for a game to be played by getting all the necessary or accustomed items in place. **3.** Having credit properly established in a casino. "Are you set up with the cage?"

"Setup on ...": A call by a dealer that fresh cards are required. "Floor, setup on 23."

7: The card with seven pips on it and the number 7. A standard deck has four such cards, one in each suit.

seven-card stud: A poker variation in which players start with two downcards and an upcard along with a betting round, then receive three more up cards and a final down card, with a betting round after each card dealt, for a total of five betting rounds. At the end, the best five-card hand wins.

seven-card stud/8: SEVEN-CARD STUD 8-OR-BETTER.

seven-card stud 8-or-better: SEVEN-CARD STUD played HIGH-LOW featuring three starting cards, two down and one up, then three successive rounds of upcards with a final seventh card dealt face down for a total of five betting rounds. To qualify for low, a player has to have five unpaired cards of 8 or less or the best high hand will win the entire pot.

seven-card stud high-low: SEVEN-CARD STUD variation in which players compete for the best high and best low hands, with each side winning half the pot.

seven-card stud high-low cards speak: SEVEN-CARD STUD HIGH-LOW in which, on the showdown, the best low hand wins the low part of the pot and the best high hand wins the high end. There is no DECLARATION and no QUALIFIER. See CARDS SPEAK.

seven-card stud high-low declare: Seven-card stud high-low in which, on the showdown, players declare whether they are going for the low end of the pot or the high (or both) to be eligible to win those sides of the pot.

seven-handed: 1. A poker game played with seven players or a game that currently has seven players seated. **2.** A pot contested by seven players.

7-nothing: In lowball or high-low, 7-4-3-2-A.

7-perfect: 7-nothing.

sevens: A pair of sevens.

seven stud high: Seven-card stud.

seventh street: In seven-card stud, the seventh and last card received along with the betting round accompanying it. Also, *river*.

shark: 1. An expert player. **2.** An unscrupulous player, one without compassion, or a crook.

sheriff: A player who calls on the river with a marginal hand because he thinks an opponent may be bluffing with a weaker hand.

shill: An individual hired by the house to play and fill a seat in a game until players fill the table. Shills play with house money, rather than their own and do not keep their winnings. Also, *game starter*. Compare to PROPOSITION PLAYER.

shoot at a player: Aggressively bet and raise at a particular player, particularly one prone to fold against aggressive betting.

shootout: 1. A game or tournament in which the winner takes all the prize money. **2.** Sometimes, specifically a single-table tournament played down to one winner. **3.** SHOOTOUT TOURNAMENT.

shootout tournament: A multiple-table tournament in which each table is played down to one winner, who then moves on to the next round, until only one player is left, the champion. Often shortened to *shootout*.

short: 1. Owe money to a pot or a player: Light. **2.** A pot that has less than the proper amount of chips in it, often part of the expression *short pot*. "Dealer, that pot is short." **3.** Not having enough money for a situation or being close to broke. **4.** A table with empty seats, one that does not have the full complement of players.

short bet: A bet that is less than the minimum amount required to open betting, or if a bet has already been made, a call or raise that is less than the size of the previous bet.

short buy: The buying of less than the customary or agreed-upon number of chips for a game.

short call: To call a bet for less than the full amount because a player doesn't have enough chips, and thus goes All in.

short game: A poker game played with less than the full complement of players. Also, *short table*. Compare to Ring game.

short-handed: A game played with less than the full or typical number of players. In hold'em, a game played with six or fewer players.

short-handed game: SHORT GAME.

short rebuy: The buying of additional chips at less than the minimum amount normally allowed.

short run: A brief sequence of trials, in which unexpected results could occur, even though the correct odds suggest that they should not. Opposite of LONG RUN.

short stack: 1. A player who has relatively few chips in comparison to opponents. **2.** A small pile of chips. **3.** In a tournament, the holder of relatively few chips compared to opponents such that the player is in serious jeopardy of losing them all.

short table: SHORT GAME.

show a hand down: Reveal cards after all the betting has been completed on the last round.

showdown: The final act of a poker hand, the point at which remaining players reveal their hands to determine the winner of the pot.

showing: The cards that are exposed and face up on the board. "Three diamonds were showing on the board."

show one, show all: A rule in cardrooms requiring a player to show all opponents his cards if he shows any one player.

show openers: Showing one's cards and proving that a pot was legitimately opened in a game that has OPENERS.

shuffle: Mixing cards so that they are arranged randomly in a deck.

shuffle in: DEAL IN.

shut down: Discontinue aggressive betting and check or sometimes fold when a SCARE CARD comes or an opponent plays back.

shut out: In a no-limit game, force or attempt to force an opponent out with a bet bigger than he is willing to call.

shy: LIGHT.

Shylock: LOAN SHARK.

side: 1. Bets or action that is not part of the main game. **2.** A separate pot created when a player is out of chips and other players are still contesting the pot. See SIDE POT.

side action: See SIDE GAME.

side bet: A bet made privately among players, one that is not part of the main action. "They had a side bet on which player would bust out first."

side card: A card that is not part of the main hand, for example, the fifth card in a two pair hand.

side game: A cash poker game played at the same time as a tournament, and sometimes filled with both weak players who bust out early and with the pros who gather like vultures to feed on the remains.

side pot: When one player has bet all his chips and two or more opponents remain, a segregated pot created for and that can only be won by players who still have chips to bet, as opposed to the MAIN POT, the collection of original bets by all active players.

sign up: 1. Register to play in a tournament. **2.** Reserve a seat for a cash game.

sign-up board: A posted list, often a blackboard or whiteboard, of players waiting for seats to open. Often shortened to *board*.

silent prop: A PROP who has not made known to his opponents that he is a house player. This is not common, because cardrooms usually require house players to wear identification clearly indicating their status.

simultaneous declaration: At the showdown in HIGH-LOW games in which players *declare* (announce) simultaneously which part of the pot they are playing for (high, low, or high and low) and can win only what they declare, as opposed to CARDS SPEAK, which is standard in cardrooms and casinos. Compare to CONSECUTIVE DECLARATION.

single add-on tournament: An ADD-ON TOURNAMENT that allows players a final purchase of one additional specified allotment of chips, usually at the end of the first few rounds of play.

single bet: One bet that is owed or made, as opposed to a DOUBLE BET. Also, *one bet*.

single-bet level: In limit poker with a two-tier structure, the first and lower level of betting that occurs in the first rounds, as opposed to *double-bet level*. For example, in a $5/$10 game, the $5 level of betting. Also *one-bet level*.

single limit: Betting structure in which all bets and raises are uniform, and no variations in bet size are allowed. For example, in a $10 single-limit draw poker game, all bets before and after the draw must be in increments of $10. Also, *straight limit*. Compare to DOUBLE LIMIT, the standard betting structure in most LIMIT GAMES.

single-suited: A hand that has possibilities of making a flush in just one suit, as opposed to DOUBLE SUITED; usually refers to a starting Omaha hand with two cards of one suit and two other cards of different suits.

single-table satellite: A one-table tournament in which the winner gains entry into a larger-buy-in tournament for a fraction of the cost. See SATELLITE TOURNAMENT. Also, *one-table satellite*.

sit-and-go: A one-table tournament that begins as soon as a table is filled; there is no scheduled starting time. Cash prizes are typically paid to the top three places. Also, *sit 'n' go, SNG*.

sit in: Join a game.

sit n' go: Sit-and-go.

sit out: Be dealt out of a game. "I'll sit out a few hands."

situational bluff: A bluff made more on the merits of a situational advantage than on positional strengths.

6: The card with six pips on it and the number 6. A standard deck has four such cards, one in each suit.

six: Sixth street.

sixes: A pair of sixes.

six-handed: 1. A poker game played with six players or a game that currently has six players seated. **2.** A pot contested by six players.

6-nothing: In lowball or high-low, 6-4-3-2-A.

6-perfect: 6-nothing.

sixthed: In a HIGH-LOW game, split either the low or high end of a pot with two other players, thus getting only one-sixth of the pot. Compare to QUARTERED, HALVED.

sixth street: In seven-card stud, the sixth card received along with the betting round accompanying it.

sixty seconds: The usual time allowance when the CLOCK is called.

six-way: A pot contested by six players.

sleep: See SLEEP A BET.

sleep a bet: 1. Miss an opportunity due to inattention. **2.** Fail to recognize that a proposition bet has been fulfilled and thus lose out on the winnings.

slow-action tournament: A tournament with levels of one hour or more.

slow down: Discontinue betting or raising by checking or calling instead.

slowplay: Bet a strong hand weakly—by checking, calling, or conservative betting—to disguise its strength and keep opponents in the pot.

slow-roll: Slowly reveal a winning hand on the end—a breach of poker etiquette considered to be offensive and rude.

small bet: 1. A bet in LIMIT POKER that is in the lower tier of the betting limit, for example, the $30 bet in a $30/$60 game. **2.** In a no-limit, pot-limit, or spread-limit game, an undersized bet, one that is less than the bet typically made in the situation.

small blind: 1. The smaller of two forced BLIND bets in flop games such as hold'em and Omaha, posted before the cards are dealt by the player immediately to the left of the BUTTON. Also called *little blind*. Compare to BIG BLIND. **2.** The player occupying this position.

small-buy-in tournament: A tournament which costs $100 or less to enter.

small card: LITTLE CARD.

small field: In a tournament, a relatively small number of players— under 100.

small-field tournament: A tournament of less than 100 players

small flush: A flush whose high card is a jack or less.

small full: In hold'em and Omaha, a full house less than the highest possible given the cards on board, for example, on a board of K-K-J-6-5, having 5-5 in the hole for a full house of 5-5-5-K-K (compared with holding K-J, for a BIG FULL of K-K-K-J-J).

small game: A game played for low limits.

small kicker: A SIDE CARD to a pair or set (or, rarely, quads) that is relatively small. For example, a player with K-K-9-5-4 holds *kings with a small kicker* (the 9).

small limit: LOW LIMIT.

small pair: A PAIR of small cards, usually sevens or less.

small suited connectors: Two cards, either the 5-4, 4-3, or 3-2, that are of consecutive rank and in the same suit.

smooth: A lowball hand with relatively strong supporting cards, for example, 8-5-3-2-A is a smooth 8, as opposed to a rough 8, such as 8-7-6-3-2.

smooth call: Call a bet when a raise would also be correct. Also, *flat call*.

smooth spot to shuffle on: Old-time poker lingo for losing all one's chips.

snakebit: 1. Having bad luck. **2.** Being afraid to make aggressive plays due to earlier losses.

snap off: 1. Call a bluffer's bet with a relatively weak hand but one that is stronger than that of the bluffer or force the bluffer to fold by betting or raising (usually with cards that are weak as well) that is, catch an opponent bluffing. **2.** Catch a card on the river to overtake and beat a hand that was ahead. **3.** Beat a big starting hand, such as aces or kings.

SNG: Sit-and-go.

snow: 1. Deceive or bluff. **2.** Represent a strong hand by betting aggressively while actually holding an inferior hand.

snowmen: In hold'em, hole cards of 8-8.

social game: Friendly game.

soft: 1. A player or game that is easy to beat. **2.** A weak player, one without good skills. **3.** Playing or betting weakly. **4.** Playing without putting pressure on opponents, checking or calling when betting or raising may be warranted. "Max always plays soft when Jill or Blue is in the pot; he doesn't like to raise against women." **5.** In a cash transaction, the amount of money the player wants back as cash, as opposed to chips. For example, a player may give a chip runner a $100 bill and ask for $50 hard (chips) and the rest soft (cash).

solid-aggressive: A player who plays only fundamentally sound hands (as opposed to speculative ones), but plays them aggressively.

solid player: A player with fundamentally good poker skills.

sophisticated: 1. A player who makes advanced or subtle plays. **2.** A situation that is played in such a manner.

south: 1. Lose or be losing. "When Joe left the cardroom, Moe went south with half the chips." **2.** Have diminishing skills. "After he got married, Manny's game went south and he would just feed chips to the other players."

space: A gap between cards in a straight draw, such as 5-7-8-9, the *space* being the gap between the 5 and 7. Also, GAP.

spaces: Cards that don't connect for good straight possibilities, that is, that have "spaces" between them, such as a flop of 4-9-Q.

spades: 1. One of the four suits in a deck of CARDS, using a black spade symbol (♠), consisting of 13 cards, 2-3-4-5-6-7-8-9-10-J-Q-K-A. **2.** An exclamation of strength. "I've got you in spades!"

speeder: A player who bets and raises excessively.

spike: 1. An ace. **2.** Catch a good card. "He spiked the third king on the turn."

spit card: In some private poker variations, an upcard shared by all players.

splash around: Play too many hands and make too many bets. "He was splashing around all evening."

splash chips: SPLASH AROUND.

splash the pot: Bet chips so that some or all land and commingle with chips already in the pot, causing it to be unclear how much was actually wagered—disallowed in poker rooms or, at the least, considered bad poker etiquette.

split agreement: An agreement to CHOP.

split game: HIGH-LOW game.

split openers: In a DRAW game with OPENING REQUIREMENTS, break up the minimum hand required to open to draw for a different hand. For example, to discard a jack from 10-J-J-Q-K to draw to 10-J-Q-K in the hopes of catching a 9 or ace for a straight.

split pair: In seven-card stud, when one card in a player's pair is held as a downcard and the other as an upcard, usually referring to the initial three-card hand.

split-out: The 50% split of profits between a house player—an "employee" hired to get another warm body into a shorthanded game—and the cardroom.

split pot: When two or more players are tied for the best hand and divide the pot evenly.

split the blinds: CHOP, definition 2.

spots: PIPS.

spread: 1. Offer a poker game. "The Horseshoe spreads seven-card stud and hold'em at the lower limit*s*." **2.** Show one's cards. "He spread a full house on the river." **3.** The difference between the minimum and the maximum bet allowed in a SPREAD-LIMIT game.

spread a hand: Reveal one's cards.

spread limit: A betting structure that allows players to bet or raise anywhere from the minimum to the maximum allowed. For example, in a $1-$5 spread-limit game, any amount between $1 and $5 can be bet or raised.

square deal: 1. A fair and honest game. **2.** A fair and honest arrangement or agreement between parties.

squared deck: A pack of cards that is perfectly arranged in one neat pile so that it looks like one unit, as opposed to a collection of roughly aligned cards.

"Square up the table": A request by a player or dealer to ensure that the middle seat is directly opposite the dealer while other chairs fanning left and right are symmetrically aligned to that central position.

squeeze: 1. Very slowly spread open one's cards for maximum dramatic effect. **2.** Put great pressure on an opponent or situation. **3.** To trap a player between two aggressive opponents. See SQUEEZED PLAYER.

squeezed player: A player caught between two aggressive bettors. One so caught might be said to be *whipsawed* or *caught in the middle*.

stack: 1. The total amount of chips a player has on the table. Also, *table bankroll*. **2.** A single pile of chips. **3.** In casinos, a unit of measurement that equals twenty chips, which is the number of chips that fit in one slot in a RACK. **4.** The total amount of chips or cash a player has. **5.** In a tournament, the relative number of chips a player has compared to other players. "After two hours of play, Ludo had the big stack at the table." **6.** Prearrange a deck or portion of a deck for purposes of manipulation or cheating. **7.** Arrange cards, cash, or chips into piles. "After winning the big pot, it took me three more hands to finish stacking my chips!"

stacked deck: A deck of cards that is prearranged by a manipulator or cheat.

stack size: 1. The total number of chips a player has on the table. **2.** The physical size of a pile of chips. **3.** In a tournament, the relative number of chips a player has compared to other players.

stake: 1. A player's bankroll. **2.** The amount of money needed to enter a game. "Joe, you're going to need a big stake to play this game, probably, $1,000." **3.** Bankroll a player in exchange for a percentage of profits or as a loan. Also *back*.

stake a player: See STAKE, definition 2.

stake player: A player (often a RAILBIRD) given chips for the purpose of getting additional players into a shorthanded game to keep it active or to help start a game. The usual arrangement is for the stake player to keep half the profits while having no penalty for losing.

stakes: The bet size in a game. "The stakes are $5/$10 and then we alternate pot limit after every round."

stand a bet: Be able to call a bet, and not have to fold.

stand a raise: Have a hand strong enough to be able to call a raise. Opposite of CAN'T STAND A RAISE.

stand pat: In DRAW POKER, take no cards at the draw. Also, *stay pat*.

standard deck: A regulation deck of 52 playing cards, with 13 cards, ace through king (A-2-3-4-5-6-7-8-9-10-J-Q-K), in each of four suits (spades, diamonds, clubs, and hearts).

standard raise: In no-limit hold'em, a typical preflop raise, usually, three times the size of the big blind.

standards of conduct: Commonly accepted etiquette for a game of poker or specific conduct rules as established by a cardroom, casino, or private host.

stand up: Have a hand hold its value and win. "My three kings looked shaky when the fourth spade hit the board, but they stood up and I took the pot."

stands to lose: 1. The amount a player can lose. "He stands to lose ten dimes in that game." **2.** A hand that seems likely to lose.

stands to win: 1. The amount a player can win. "He stands to win a bundle in that game." **2.** A hand that seems likely to win.

stare down: Use a withering or intimidating stare as a form of bullying or as a way to elicit a TELL in a crucial situation, for example, when an opponent has made an all-in bet.

starter: GAME STARTER.

◆

starting cards: The initial cards dealt to a player. In hold'em, these are the first two cards and in Omaha, the first four cards (and known in both games as *pocket cards* or *hole cards*). In draw poker, these are the first five cards and in seven-card stud variations, the initial three cards.

starting hand: STARTING CARDS.

starting hand selection: The initial cards a player normally considers worthy of play.

starting requirements: STARTING HAND SELECTION.

start the action: Make the first bet.

stay pat: STAND PAT.

steal: Bet or raise with an inferior hand that would probably lose if played to the showdown, with the goal of forcing opponents to fold so that the pot can be won by default.

steal position: The dealer's position (BUTTON) or the seat before (CUTOFF), strategically good positions from which to raise an unraised pot, attempt to force opponents into folding, and win the blinds or antes by default.

steal the antes: On the first round of betting, bluff opponents out of a pot no one has entered so that the antes can be won without a fight.

steal the blinds: On the first round of betting, bluff opponents out of a pot no one has entered so that the blinds (and antes, if any) can be won without a fight.

steam: Be angry or upset after having lost a big pot or succession of pots and play recklessly as a result. Also, be ON TILT.

steam bet: A bet that a player would ordinarily not make except that he is STEAMING.

steamer: A player on tilt.

steaming: ON TILT.

steerer: An individual who hustles players into a game, typically referring to tough or crooked games.

step out: Make a big bet in a pot-limit or no-limit game.

stiff: 1. Not tip in a situation in which tipping is customary. "Gradson stiffed the dealer after winning that big pot." **2.** A player who is not skilled and thus easily beat.

stone cold bluff: A bet made with the intention of forcing all opponents to fold, one which has almost no chance of winning if called.

stone cold nuts: The best possible hand, given the situation.

straddle: 1. Before the cards are dealt, an optional raise for two times the big blind made by the player seated to his left, which gives the straddler the option of last action on the first round of betting. Often called *live straddle*. **2.** Formerly, a term used for the second blind bet in a two-blind game that used to be called *a blind and straddle game*.

straggler: A player who enters the pot cheaply, usually from a late position.

straight: A poker hand consisting of five consecutive cards of mixed suits, such as 4-5-6-7-8 or 10-J-Q-K-A. A straight may not "wrap" around the ace, so Q-K-A-2-3 is not a straight, but merely an ace-high hand.

straight card: A card that makes a straight.

straight draw: 1. Three or four cards to a possible straight, such as 4-5-7 or 8-9-10-J. **2.** DRAW POKER played high only, as opposed to LOWBALL or HIGH-LOW.

straight flush: A poker hand consisting of five consecutive cards in the same suit, such as 7♦ 8♦ 9♦ 10♦ J♦, called a *jack-high straight flush*. A straight-flush may not wrap around the ace, thus K♦ A♦ 2♦ 3♦ 4♦ is not a straight-flush, but an ace-high diamond flush.

straight flush draw: Three or four cards to a possible straight flush, such as J-Q-K or 8-9-10-J, all in the same suit.

straight limit: SINGLE LIMIT.

streak: 1. An uninterrupted succession of winning or losing hands or sessions. **2.** A greater number of winning or losing sessions than would ordinarily be expected.

street: In stud and flop games, a betting round marked by a new card or cards being dealt.

string bet: Additional chips added to a bet that has already been placed, that is, a player's hand has been removed from the chips wagered, making such bet official and final (unless declared otherwise verbally). String bets are disallowed in all public poker games.

strip poker: Poker played for clothes, rather than chips. This is the only poker variation whose goal is for all players to lose all their currency, that is, their clothes!.

strong ace: An ace accompanied by a high SIDE CARD, such as a jack, queen, or king.

strong hand: A hand likely to win.

structure: 1. In tournaments, the predetermined format, including the number of levels, how often the levels increase, the blinds and antes for each level, and the division of the prize pool. **2.** In cash games, the preset betting limits.

structured limit: A game in which the betting amounts are constrained, for example a $5/$10 game, in which all bets and raises must be exactly $5 until a specified point and exactly $10 after that point.

stuck: 1. A player who is losing. "I'm stuck." **2.** The amount of money a player is losing. "I'm stuck $2,100 in that game."

stud: STUD POKER.

stud player: 1. A player who plays stud poker. **2.** Any skilled poker player. (In some contexts, this broad usage applies to poker players in general and not specifically to those who play stud poker.)

stud poker: A poker variation in which some of the cards in each player's hand are dealt face up and some face down. For example, SEVEN-CARD STUD (three downcards, four upcards) and FIVE-CARD STUD (one downcard, four upcards).

sucker: 1. An individual who is easily induced into scams or situations he is unlikely to win. **2.** A mark for hustlers. **3.** A bad player. **4.** Live one.

suck it up: 1. Fold a hand against heavy betting and take a big loss even though it is suspected that an opponent is bluffing. **2.** Accept adversity without complaint.

suck out: Have a big underdog hand that wins on the last or next-to-last card. Similar to Draw out, but with the connotation of a more miraculous turnaround. "Philly caught the miracle 9 for the full house and sucked out on the river."

suicide king: K♥, so named for the sword pointing at his own head.

suit: One of the four classes of playing cards, hearts (♥), spades (♠), diamonds (♦), and clubs (♣), that make up a full deck.

suited: Pertaining to two or more cards in the same suit.

suited connectors: Cards that are of consecutive rank and in the same suit, such as 8♥ 9♥.

suited up: Having two or more cards in the same suit.

supernit: An extremely tight player who plays only premium hands, and is thus, very predictable. Compare to NIT.

supersatellite: A low buy-in tournament featuring multiple tables, in which the top finishers win seats into a large-buy-in tournament for a fraction of the cost. For example, $200 supersatellites typically precede $10,000 events and allow players with smaller bankrolls to earn a shot at the big event.

Super System: Two-time world champion Doyle Brunson's classic guide to winning at poker, written in 1978. A companion volume was published in 2005. These two books are considered the bibles of the game and the greatest poker books ever written.

Super System 2: The 2005 follow-up to Doyle Brunson's SUPER SYSTEM.

surrender the pot: Fold.

survival tactics: Playing in a manner that affords the best chance to last longer in a tournament without elimination, with a greater emphasis on conservative risk-free play as opposed to aggressive play.

sweat a player: Cheer on a competitor. "When Bobby T. made the final table, we went down to the Bellagio to sweat him."

sweeten the pot: Put another bet or raise into the pot.

swing shift: Afternoon to evening shift. Also *p.m.*

switch gears: CHANGE GEARS.

T: Symbol used in written text for a 10 in any suit.

tab card: A card held by the house that shows markers and credits advanced to players.

table: POKER TABLE.

table bankroll: **1.** The total number of chips a player has on the table. **2.** The amount of money a player has set aside for a session of play.

table change: In a tournament or cash game, when a player is assigned or moves to another table.

table charge: **1.** TIME, definition 2. **2.** RAKE.

table image: The way a player's betting patterns are viewed by opponents, as aggressive, conservative, tight, passive, or some combination of these.

table stakes: The rule, common in all public cardrooms and most private games, that a player's bet or call of a bet is limited to the amount of money he has on the table in front of him.

take: 1. The house percentage, specifically, in poker, the RAKE.
2. Draw a card in DRAW POKER. "I'll take three cards."

take a bath: Lose very heavily.

take a card off: Call a bet so that another card can be seen. Also, *take off a card, take one off.*

take a piece of: Finance part of a player's bankroll and take a percentage of his profits.

take a shot: Play a speculative hand or enter into a speculative situation.

take a stab at: Bet hoping that opponents will fold or another card can be seen without a raise.

take down a pot: Win a hand and the chips in the middle.

take him off his game: Play in a manner that throws off an opponent and forces him to adapt to a style of play he is not comfortable with.

take it down: 1. Win a pot. **2.** Words said by a player when he folds to let his opponent know that he's won the hand.

"Take it, Doyle": A classic line from Doyle Brunson's magnum opus, *Super System*, wherein Doyle describes his opponents' words when they consistently fold against his aggressive betting.

take off a card: Take a card off.

take one off: Take a card off.

take the lead: Lead, definition 1.

take the worst of it: See worst of it.

talking chips: Winnings.

tall stack: 1. A player who has a lot of chips. **2.** The player with the most chips at his table. "Benny's the tall stack at the table."

tank: See INTO THE TANK.

tap city: A player who is or has gone broke. Also, *tapped out*.

tap out:, Go broke at the table.

tapped out: TAP CITY.

television bubble: In a televised tournament, the point at which all players will make the final table, which will be broadcast, except for the next player to bust out. See BUBBLE.

television table: A table that television cameras are filming, either a featured game before the final table or the final table itself.

tell: An inadvertent mannerism or reaction that reveals information about the strength of a player's hand.

10: The card with ten pips on it and the number 10. A standard deck has four such cards, one in each suit.

Ten-handed: **1.** A poker game played with ten players or a game that currently has ten players seated. **2.** A pot contested by ten players.

Tens: A pair of tens.

Ten seconds: The final ten-second warning a player gets to act on his hand or be automatically folded when the CLOCK is called.

terminator: In a tournament, a player who eliminates an opponent from play.

Texas Hold'em: HOLD'EM.

the nuts: See NUTS.

there: Having made a particular hand. "The straight didn't fill on the turn, but I got there on the river." Also see BEING THERE.

think tank: See INTO THE TANK.

third draw: In TRIPLE DRAW, the third exchange of unwanted cards for new ones.

third of a bet: The difference in size between the big blind and the small blind bet in a TWO-AND-THREE CHIP BLIND STRUCTURE. "In a two-and-three chip structure, such as a $15/$30 game with blinds of $10 and $15, it is generally correct for the little blind to call a third of a bet in an unraised pot because the cost is so little."

third pair: In flop games, a pair formed by combining a pocket card with the third-highest board card. On the flop, this would also be known as BOTTOM PAIR.

third street: In seven-card stud, the first betting round, named for the three cards held by each player.

3: The card with three pips on it and the number 3. A standard deck has four such cards, one in each suit.

three: THIRD STREET, the first betting round in seven-card stud. "From the button, he raised on three."

three-bet: Raise a raise, making it three bets total.

◆

three bets: A bet and two raises in a round. "Daugherty bet, McEvoy raised and Cloutier made it three bets." Compare with ONE BET, when only a single bet is owed or made. Also see TWO BETS, FOUR BETS.

three-card draw: In DRAW POKER variations, the exchange of three unwanted cards on the draw for three new ones.

three-card monte: 1. A con game played with three cards, often associated with urban street hustlers using sleight of hand to separate marks from their money **2.** A poker variation played with three cards.

three-handed: 1. A poker game played with three players or a game that currently has three players seated. **2.** A pot contested by three players.

three of a kind: A poker hand containing three cards of the same rank, such as 4-4-4, called *three fours*. Also *set*, *trips*, *triplets*.

three-quartered: In a HIGH-LOW game, win either the high or low outright, and tie an opponent for the other half of the pot, thereby winning three-fourths of the entire pot.

threes: A pair of threes.

three-way: A pot contested by three players.

throw a party: Lose heavily, the connotation being that the loser is showering money on the other players.

throw off (chips or money): Make bad bets and foolishly "toss" away money or chips.

ticket: 1. A card. "Deal me a ticket." **2.** An excellent card or hand. "Manny had the right ticket for the pot."

tied into the pot: Committed to a hand, right to the showdown.

tight: 1. A player who plays only premium hands and enters few pots. **2.** When applied to a game, a collection of players who play few pots and give little action.

tight-aggressive: A player who plays few hands, but when he does, he plays them aggressively.

tilt: See ON TILT.

time: TIME COLLECTION.

"Time!": 1. A player's request or an announcement that he needs more time to deliberate on his hand. **2.** An announcement by the cardroom alerting players that they need to pay the TIME COLLECTION.

time bank: An online poker term that refers to a cache of time from which a player can draw automatically if he has not responded in a prescribed time.

time collection: The fee a cardroom collects at regularly intervals (often hourly) from players to play poker. Compare with RAKE.

time collector: The employee who collects the house fees for games that have a TIME COLLECTION.

timed out: An online poker term for a hand that automatically loses when a player doesn't bet in the required amount of time.

tip: A gratuity given by a player to an employee for services performed. Often called *toke* in casinos.

tip off: Display a mannerism or style of play (a TELL) that alerts an opponent to the strength of one's hand.

tip your hand: Alert opponents to a hand's strength by the way the hand is bet or by a physical TELL.

to go: The amount of a bet made that opponents must call to continue playing the hand. "Frankie pushed out some chips and announced, 'That will be $400 to go.'"

toke: Casino parlance for TIP.

tom: A bad tipper.

"Too rich for my blood": An expression indicating that a bet or raise is too expensive and the player is folding.

top and bottom pair: In hold'em and Omaha, having one's hole cards pair the highest card on the flop and the lowest card. For example, hold K-4 in hold'em on a flop of K-Q-4, for kings and fours.

top end of a straight: In hold'em and Omaha, the part of the straight that is the highest possible given the cards on the board, for example, holding a 10 with a board of 6-7-8-9 when an opponent might be holding the low or IGNORANT END OF A STRAIGHT, a 5.

top hand: 1. The best hand. **2.** The winning hand.

top kicker: 1. The side card to a pair, two pair, three of a kind, or quad hand being higher than the side card of an opponent with an equivalently ranked hand. For example, with a board of K-J-8-7-2, if you have A-K and your opponent has K-T, you both have two kings, but your ace is the top kicker. **2.** The side card being the highest possible card, usually an ace.

top off: The British term for ADD ON.

top pair: 1. In flop games, a pocket card that combines with the highest board card to form a pair. **2.** Having a higher-ranked pair than an opponent.

top set: In FLOP GAMES, the best possible THREE OF A KIND formed by combining the pocket cards with the highest board card. Also, *overset*.

top straight: 1. The best straight possible given the board cards.
2. Having a higher straight than an opponent.

top two pair: In hold'em and Omaha, pocket cards that combine with the two highest board cards. For example, in hold'em, A-J on an A-J-9-3-2 board forms the top two pair of aces and jacks.

top wrap: In Omaha, a draw to the high end of a straight on a hand with more than eight cards that will fill the straight. For example, with hole cards of 9-8-6-x and a flop of Q-7-5, any 9, 8, 6, or 4 makes a straight. Compare with BOTTOM WRAP.

total entries: The number of players in a tournament.

total prize pool: PRIZE POOL.

tough: A game or player that is difficult to beat.

tournament: A competition among players who typically start with an equal number of chips and play until one player holds all the chips or, in certain tournaments, until a specified number of players remain. Players compete for prizes, typically cash, and get eliminated when they run out of chips. See REBUY TOURNAMENT and ADD-ON TOURNAMENT, events that allow players to purchase additional chips for a specified period of time, usually the first two or three rounds of play.

tournament chips: CHIPS used only for tournaments and that have no cash value.

tournament director: The supervisor responsible for handling disputes, and organizing and running a tournament.

tournament player: 1. A poker player who competes in tournaments or is playing in a tournament. **2.** A derogatory term used by cash players for players who are proficient in tournament play but cannot win in the "real" cash games.

tourney: TOURNAMENT.

trail: 1. Have a weaker hand than an opponent with more cards to be drawn. **2.** Call bets after one or more players have already called.

trap: Induce a player to invest more money in a situation in which he is an almost sure loser.

trapped: CAUGHT IN THE MIDDLE.

trash: 1. Worthless cards or a hand with little potential for winning. **2.** Get rid of cards; MUCK.

traveling blinds: BLINDS that move by position, clockwise around the table—this is the typical structure in hold'em and Omaha games—rather than being posted by the previous winner.

tray: RACK.

trey: A 3 (the card).

tricky play: Checking, betting, or raising in a situation that seems contrary to the apparent or logical play, with the purpose of fooling opponents into thinking one has a hand of a different nature.

triple ante: When the antes in two successive unopened pots are applied to a third deal along with a new ante such that each player has anted thrice.

triple bet: 1. A bet and two raises that are owed or made. **2.** Three bets, as opposed to a single bet, where only one bet is owed or made, or a double bet, where two are made.

triple draw: Five card draw LOWBALL with three separate draws in which players get to replace unwanted cards with new ones, and with four rounds of betting (as opposed to the two in traditional draw poker). Triple draw is often played DEUCE-TO-SEVEN.

triple raise: A raise and two reraises in a round.

triple through: Triple one's chips on a single hand (at the expense of two opponents with larger stacks) or in a session.

triplets: THREE OF A KIND.

trips: THREE OF A KIND.

trivial fold: Opting out of play with a very weak hand, one with no good draw possibilities and no pair or better.

trouble hand: A hand that, if played incorrectly, can lead to disastrous losses.

true odds: When the payout on a bet is exactly equally to the likelihood of that event occurring.

tuna: 1. Weak player. **2.** Sucker.

turkey: A bird fit for picking, that is, a player with weak skills; a PRODUCER or FISH.

turn: 1. In modern usage, the fourth community card in flop games such as Omaha and Texas hold'em. Also *fourth street*. **2.** In earlier usage, pre-1980s, the term for what is nowadays known as the FLOP, that is, the simultaneous dealing of three cards after the first betting round in hold'em and Omaha. **3.** The point at which it is a player's turn to act, deal, or receive cards in a game.

turn down: Fold.

turned: 1. A hand made on the turn, as in *he turned a set* or *a straight flush*. **2.** A card that is dealt or drawn, as in *a 7♦ turned on the river and I was busted.*

"Turn one": "RUN 'EM."

2: 1. The card with two pips on it and the number 2. A standard deck has four such cards, one in each suit.

two-and-four-chip blind structure: A BLIND structure in which two chips are used for the small blind and four for the big blind, as in a $20/$40 game, which has blinds of $10 (two $5 chips) and $20 (four $5 chips). Compare with ONE-AND-TWO-CHIP BLIND STRUCTURE.

two-and-three chip-blind structure: A BLIND structure in which the small blind is two-thirds the size of the big blind, as in a $15/$30 game, which has blinds of $10 (two $5 chips) and $15 (three $5 chips).

two-bet: Raise a bettor, making it two bets total.

two-bet level: DOUBLE-BET LEVEL.

two bets: A bet and a raise in a round, as opposed to ONE BET. "After the bet and the raise, it was two bets to Todd." Also see THREE BETS, FOUR BETS.

two bets cold: A bet and a raise to be called by a player who has not yet entered the pot in the round.

two-card draw: In DRAW POKER variations, the exchange of two unwanted cards on the draw for two new ones.

two-dimensional: In HIGH-LOW poker, a hand that can win both the high and low ends of the pot, as opposed to ONE DIMENSIONAL.

two flush: Two cards in the same suit.

two-gap: A nonconsecutive straight draw with two holes, such as 9-10-K, or, in a game using more than five cards, a hand such as 4-5-7-8-10-J to which one of two cards, the 6 or 9, can be drawn to form a straight. Also DOUBLE BELLY BUSTER, DOUBLE GAPPER.

two-handed: HEAD TO HEAD.

two pair: A poker hand containing two sets of two cards of the same rank, such as A-A-5-5, called *aces and fives*.

two-straight: Two consecutive cards, such as 7-8 or 10-J.

two table satellite: A SATELLITE TOURNAMENT consisting of two tables.

two-way: 1. Two players competing for a pot. **2.** In HIGH-LOW games, a hand that can go both high and low.

twos: A pair of twos.

uncoordinated board: A board in Omaha or hold'em that has no flush or straight draws, such as Q-7-3 or 10-5-2 of three suits.

underbet: In NO-LIMIT or POT-LIMIT poker, bet less than a standard amount in a given situation, either to entice opponents to put more money into a pot they're going to lose, anticipate being able to reraise and get more money into a pot, or enter a pot cheaply.

undercall: At the showdown, announce a hand as being of less value than it is what is actually held, for example, announcing one pair when a two pair hand is held, either as an honest mistake or sometimes to NEEDLE an opponent. Compare with OVERCALL, MISCALL.

underdog: 1. A hand or situation that is likely to lose or perceived to be likely to lose; as opposed to FAVORITE. **2.** An event that is mathematically unlikely to occur **3.** A bet that pays more per unit in winnings than is risked. For example, when betting against a 2 to 1 favorite, the bettor who takes the underdog risks $1 to win $2. Also, *dog*.

underfull: In hold'em and Omaha, a full house in which the three of a kind portion combines with other than the highest-ranking board card such that a higher full house is possible. For example, in hold'em, if the board is J-J-A-5-4, a player holding A-J (for a hand of three jacks and two aces) has an *underfull* compared to someone holding A-A (for a hand of three aces and two jacks), which is called an OVERFULL.

underpair: In hold'em and Omaha, a pocket pair that is smaller than any open card on the board. For example, 5-5 on a flop of 9-J-Q. Compare with OVERPAIR.

underset: In hold'em and Omaha, THREE OF A KIND formed by combining the pocket cards with other than the highest board card (and which loses to a higher-ranking three of a kind hand formed with a higher card on board).

under the gun: The first player to act in a round of poker, particularly the first betting round.

unit: Bet size used as a standard measurement. For example, in a $5/$10 game, the unit size is $5, with the larger bets, the $10 ones, being a two-unit bet. If a player loses $100 in a session, it could also be expressed as losing 20 units.

unlimited rebuy tournament: A REBUY TOURNAMENT that allows players to purchase additional chips as often as they get broke during a specified period of time, usually, the first three rounds or first few hours. Compare to MULTIPLE REBUY TOURNAMENT.

unmade hand: Cards that need improvement to form a good and probable winning hand, for example, in a high game, a four-flush, which is one card short of completing, or in ACE-TO-FIVE, 7-5-4-3, which needs another BABY to form a good low.

unmatched card: A card that doesn't work well in connection with others to form straight or flush possibilities. DANGLER.

unplayable: A situation or hand that is so disadvantageous in which it would be grossly unprofitable to bet or call any bets that are made.

unraised pot: 1. A hand in which there were no raises in the first round of betting. **2.** A round with no raises yet made.

unsuited: Cards of different suits. See OFFSUIT.

unsuited connectors: Cards that are of consecutive rank, such as 8-9, but are not of the same suit, such as an 8♥ 9♦. Compare with SUITED CONNECTORS.

up: 1. A card dealt or showing with its pips exposed so that its value can be viewed by all players. **2.** Winning. "Jackie's up about two grand." **3.** The higher pair in a two pair hand, as J-J-10-10-6 is called *jacks up* or 8-8-3-3-K is called *eights up.* **4.** Raise. "Let's up that $500."

upcard: A card that can be viewed by all players.

up front: In early position. Also, *in front.*

up to: Pertaining to whose turn it is to act. "It's up to Frank." "Who's it up to?"

user name: HANDLE.

value: 1. A hand with winning potential. **2.** A bet made to increase the pot when a hand has winning potential. **3.** The present or future worth (usually positive) of a card or situation. **4.** To create more betting action for a hand that may win.

value bet: A wager made for the purpose of increasing the pot—as opposed to having opponents fold—with either the best cards, cards that have a good chance of winning but may not be the best, or a drawing hand that would likely win if completed.

verbal bet: ORAL BET.

vig: VIGORISH.

vigorish: A percentage edge either built into a bet or charged as a fixed amount or charged by the hand or per hour by a cardroom, casino, or bookie, as its fee for spreading a game or hosting a wager.

vulnerable: A hand that is susceptible to getting beat.

wager: 1. A bet. **2.** A proposition.

wages: A poker player's estimated or desired average winnings over a period of time, often one day. "How'd you do today?" "I made wages."

wake up with a hand: To be dealt strong starting cards.

wash: SCRAMBLE.

weak ace: An ace accompanied by a low SIDE CARD, such as a 5 or 7.

weak bet: 1. A wager that appears to represent and suggest a marginal or weak hand. **2.** A small-sized bet.

weak lead: An overly small bet made by the first or second player to act, that suggests, but may not necessarily be, weakness in his hand.

welsher: A player who fails to make good on a debt.

"We're on": A statement verifying that a proposition is agreed to.

whale: A gambler who plays for very high stakes.

---

wheel: 1. In low poker, the best hand possible; in ACE-TO-FIVE, A-2-3-4-5; in DEUCE-TO-SEVEN, 2-3-4-5-7 that is not a flush. **2.** In high poker, a five-high straight.

wheel cards: 1. In low or high-low ACE-TO-FIVE, any of the cards ace to 5. **2.** In low or high-low DEUCE-TO-SEVEN, any of the cards, 2, 3, 4, 5, or 7, which can be used to form a wheel. **3.** In high poker any of the cards ace to 5.

wheel draw: In low or high-low games, a hand containing three or four of the cards needed for the best possible low hand; in ACE-TO-FIVE, those cards are A, 2, 3, 4, and 5; in DEUCE-TO-SEVEN, 2, 3, 4, 5, and 7.

where a player is at: Betting or raising for the specific purpose of seeing how an opponent will react—call, raise, or fold—so that his relative hand strength can be deduced.

whipsawed: Being trapped between a bettor and a raiser.

white-chip game: A small-stakes poker game, played with white chips, the standard color for $1 chips in many casinos.

white meat: The profit from a session.

"Who's it on?": In a game, asking whose turn it is to ACT.

wide open: Playing aggressive or reckless poker, usually due to being upset over a bad loss. Also, ON TILT.

wild: A WILD CARD, as in DEUCES WILD.

wild card: A card that can be given any rank or value by its holder, even as a duplicate of a card already held by another player.

wild-card poker: Poker games using WILD CARDS.

win: 1. Have the best hand and receive the money in the pot. **2.** Finish first in a tournament, event, or competition. **3.** Earn money in a cash game or tournament.

window: CAGE.

winner: 1. The player who has the best hand. **2.** The player who finishes first in a tournament. **3.** One who makes money playing poker **4.** A person who is viewed as successful either in earning money or overall as a class act or competitor.

winner blind: A form of KILL GAME in which the winner of a hand posts a BLIND on the next hand.

winning hand: The hand that wins the pot before the showdown or the best hand at the showdown.

winning streak: A series of plays or sessions that result in frequent or consecutive wins and good success. Also GOOD RUN, *hot streak*. Opposite of LOSING STREAK.

wired: 1. A pair in the player's pocket cards. **2.** In stud, a SPLIT PAIR. **3.** Consecutively dealt cards of the same rank.

Woolworth: In hold'em, hole cards of 5-10, named for the chain's one-time five-and-dime discounted items.

working: Cards that coordinate with one another such that there are good straight or flush possibilities.

World Championship of Poker: The $10,000-buy-in no-limit hold'em main event at the WORLD SERIES OF POKER, acknowledged as the official and accepted world championship of poker.

world-class: A player or an event that is among the best in the world.

World Poker Tour: The televised poker tour formed in 2002 by visionaries Steve Lipscomb and Lyle Berman, which has revolutionized and invigorated the modern game of poker.

World's Fair: 1. A very powerful hand. **2.** The NUTS.

World Series of Poker: The World Championship of Poker previously run by the Binion family and held every year from 1970-2004 at the Horseshoe Casino in Las Vegas (since taken over by Harrah's Entertainment and moved to a different Las Vegas venue).

worst of it: 1. Having a worse hand than opponents in a situation, one that will be unprofitable in the long run. Often part of the phrase *have, get,* or *take the worst of it.* **2.** Having a losing hand.

WPT: WORLD POKER TOUR.

wrap: In Omaha, a straight draw with more than eight cards that will complete it, for example, holding 8-9-10-K with a board of 3-6-7, a hand with 13 outs—four fives, and three each of eights, nines, and 10s. Also called *wraparound*.

wraparound: Wrap.

wraparound straight draw: Wrap.

WSOP: World Series of Poker.

x: Symbol used to indicate cards that are irrelevant to a hand or situation. "He started with pocket queens and the board came Q-x-x."

"You're good": What one player says to another when the opponent's hand is the winner. "I've got nothing, you're good."

"You're short": A reminder that a player owes money to a pot or has insufficient antes or blinds posted.

"You're up": A reminder to a player that it is his turn to act.

Basics of 11 Poker Variations

—Quick Game Capsules—

Your object in poker is to win the money in the **pot,** the accumulation of bets and antes gathered in the center of the table. In all poker variations, you can win the pot in two ways:

- By having the best hand at the **showdown**—the final act in poker, the point at which all active players' hands are revealed to see who has the best one.
- By forcing out all opponents through bets and raises they won't match.

Note that the **betting structures**—whether the game is played **limit** (in a two-tier structure such as $5-$10), **no-limit** (with all your chips at risk in any one hand), or **pot-limit** (in which your maximum bet can be up to the size of the pot)—don't change the way any of the poker variations are played, only the amount of money that can be bet.

Following are quick capsules on how the standard major games of poker are played.

—Texas Hold'em—

Texas hold'em, or just **hold'em** as the game is more commonly called, is played as high poker, that is, the player with the best (highest) five-card combination at the showdown has the winning hand and collects the money in the pot.

Your final five-card hand in hold'em is made up of *any* combination of the seven cards available to you, the five community cards dealt face up in the middle of the table (called the **board**—cards shared by all players), and the two cards you are dealt face down (your **pocket cards** or **hole cards**, which you alone can use). For example, your final hand could be made up of your two pocket cards and three cards from the board, one of your pocket cards and four from the board, or simply all five board cards.

The **action** starts with each player getting dealt two face-down cards. There is a betting round, with each player, getting a chance to exercise his options of betting. Then three cards are dealt simultaneously on the table for all **active** (remaining) players to share. This is called the **flop**, and It is followed by another round of betting. A fourth board card, called the **turn** or **fourth street**, is then dealt, and it, too, is followed with a round of betting. One final community card is dealt in the center of the table, making five cards total. This is called the **river** or **fifth street**, and it is followed by the fourth and final betting round.

Hold'em is played with a **button** (a disk that indicates the **dealer position** and that moves clockwise around the table after each deal), as well as a **small blind** and a **big blind**. The first betting round starts with the player immediately to the left of the big blind. Since there is already a bet in the middle (the big blind) this first player must call that bet to stay active, or he must fold. Of course, he can raise as well if he likes. Each player in turn then has the same three choices: fold, call, raise. In succeeding rounds, the betting action starts with the first active player to the left of the button.

When all the betting has concluded, if two or more players remain, there is the **showdown**, in which the highest-ranking hand wins the **pot** (the accumulation of bets that are kept in the center of the table).

—Omaha—

Omaha, which is also called **Omaha high**, is a high poker game that is played exactly like hold'em, except for two differences:

- Players get *four* cards to start with, as opposed to just two as in hold'em.
- Each player *must* use exactly two of his pocket cards, not more, not less, together with three from the board, to form his final five-card hand.

Omaha is played with a button, which moves clockwise around the table after each deal, as well as a small blind and a big blind. The action starts with each player getting four downcards, called **pocket cards**. The first betting round proceeds exactly as in hold'em, with the player to the left of the big blind acting first. When the betting action has been completed on the preflop round, the **flop** of three community cards is turned face up in the center of the table. This is followed by a round of betting. The **turn** and **river** are similarly dealt, each followed by a betting round. At the showdown, the highest hand wins the pot.

Omaha High-Low 8-or-Better

Omaha can also be played as high-low in a variation called **Omaha high-low 8-or-better** or, simply, **Omaha 8-or-better**. In this version, the best low hand and best high hand split the pot, however, if no hand **qualifies** for low, the best high hand **scoops** (wins the entire pot). Players can choose two different sets of cards to make their final hands, one set for the high hand and one set for the low hand. The best high and low hand can be held by the same player; if so, that player also scoops.

In 8-or-better, there is a requirement that the best low hand must have five unpaired cards of 8 or lower to win the low half of the pot. If no low meets that qualification, then the best high hand scoops the entire pot.

—Draw Poker—

In draw poker variations, each player is dealt five face-down cards to start and there are two betting rounds. The first one occurs after the initial cards are received and before the **draw**, when players have an opportunity to exchange unwanted cards for new ones. In cardroom draw poker, players may exchange up to five cards. (In some home games, players are restricted to drawing three cards, unless they have an ace and can draw four cards to it, but this is unusual.) The second round of betting occurs after the draw. At the showdown, the highest hand wins the pot. If all other players have folded, the last remaining player is the winner.

Draw poker is sometimes played with an **ante**, a mandatory bet placed by all players before the cards are dealt, and sometimes with a **blind**, a mandatory bet placed by two players (sometimes three, sometimes only one). Sometimes, rarely, both a blind bet and an ante are used as part of the structure.

Draw Poker: Jacks or Better

To open the betting in jacks or better, a player must have a hand with a minimum ranking of a pair of jacks (called **openers**). Any player, even one with openers, can elect not to open. Once an opening bet is made, subsequent players can call, fold, or raise the opener. Checking is no longer permitted. If all players check on the opening round of play, the hand is said to be **passed out**. If that occurs, the cards are collected and shuffled, and the next player in turn gets the dealer's position. In any hand in which there is betting, after the first round of betting is completed, there is a draw, which is followed by a second round of betting, and then the showdown.

Draw Poker: Anything Opens

This game is played similarly to jacks or better, except that *any* hand can open the betting, regardless of strength. For example, a pair of sevens could open the betting in the *anything opens* game, or even a queen-high hand. Otherwise the rules and methods of play are identical to jacks or better.

Draw Poker: Lowball

In lowball, the *lowest* hand is the best, as opposed to high poker games in which the highest hand is the best. In the **ace-to-five** version of lowball, the ace counts as the *lowest* card of a hand. The 2 is the next lowest card, and therefore the next best lowball card, and is followed in rank by the 3, 4, 5, and so on up to the king, which is the worst card. The highest card counts in determining the value of a hand; the lower the highest card, the better the hand. For example, 7-6-4-2-A is better than 8-4-3-2-A (known as an 8-4 or 8-high). When the top cards of competing hands are equivalent, the next-highest cards are compared to determine the winner. Thus, the hand 9-6-5-2-A beats 9-6-5-4-A.

The **wheel** or **bicycle**, 5-4-3-2-A, is the perfect lowball hand. 6-4-3-2-A is the next-strongest lowball hand, followed in order by 6-5-3-2-A, 6-5-4-2-A, 6-5-4-3-A, 6-5-4-3-2, 7-4-3-2-A, 7-5-3-2-A, and so on. In ace-to-five lowball, straights and flushes do not count against the low hand. A wheel, 5-4-3-2-A, is not considered a straight and 8-4-3-2-A, all of hearts is simply an 8-4 hand, not a flush as it would be in high poker. Pairs are also bad in lowball. Thus, the otherwise poor hand K-Q-J-10-7 is better than 4-3-2-A-A. Any unpaired hand beats any hand that contains a pair. Any hand with one pair beats any hand with two pair, and so on.

Lowball, like hold'em and Omaha, uses a button to mark the dealer position, and is usually played with three blinds, a dealer blind, small blind, and big blind, to stimulate action. Sometimes lowball is played with just two blinds, a small blind and big blind.

A version of lowball called **deuce-to-seven** does count straights and flushes against the low hand. In that game, the lowest and best card is a deuce and the highest, and therefore worst card, is an ace. So the best hand is 7-5-4-3-2 of mixed suits, with 7-6-4-3-2, 7-6-5-3-2, and 7-6-5-4-2 being the next three best hands. Since straights and flushes are bad hands, 7-6-5-4-3 and A-6-5-4-3 are beaten by the "lowly" hand of K-Q-J-9-8. And a 7-5-4-3-2 hand in clubs, a flush, loses to 4-4-4-K-J!

Triple Draw

As implied by its name, triple draw has three separate draws in which players can replace unwanted cards with new ones. As opposed to the other draw poker variations, in which there are just two betting rounds, one before the draw and one after, triple draw features four betting rounds—one when the cards are dealt, and one after each successive draw. Because of the number of cards needed, triple draw is played by a maximum of six players.

Triple draw, like hold'em and Omaha, uses a button to mark the dealer position, and is played with a small blind and big blind to stimulate action. Sometimes triple draw is played with three blinds, a dealer blind, small blind, and big blind.

Triple draw is often played as **deuce-to-seven** low, whose hand rankings are described in the previous section.

—Seven-Card Stud—

Seven-card stud's three main variations—high, low, and high-low—pack five exciting betting rounds into play. In each variation, players form their best five-card combination out of the seven cards dealt to produce their final hands.

After the first three cards are dealt, two face-down (closed) and one face-up (open), the first betting round commences. The following three cards—the fourth, fifth and sixth—are dealt open, one at a time, to each active player, with a betting round following each card. The last card, the seventh, comes face down, giving each active player three downcards and four upcards. A final round of betting follows the seventh card, and then the showdown occurs, with the best hand (or hands, as may be the case in the high-low version), winning the pot.

Seven-Card Stud High
In **seven-card stud high**, the highest ranking hand remaining wins the pot. That hand is determined by using the best five among a player's seven cards.

Seven-Card Stud Low (Razz)

In **seven-card stud low** (also called **razz**), the lowest hand, using ace-to-five rankings, wins the pot. That hand is determined by using the best five among a player's seven cards.

Seven-card Stud High-Low

In **seven-card stud high-low** (and its variant, **seven card stud 8-or-better**), players vie for either the highest-ranking or lowest-ranking hand, with the best of each claiming half the pot. Those hands are determined by using the best five among a player's seven cards. Players can choose two different sets of cards to make their final hands, one set for the high hand and one set for the low hand. The best high and low hand can be held by the same player; if so, that player also **scoops**.

Seven-Card Stud High-Low 8-or-Better

Seven-card high-low stud is sometimes played with a requirement, called a **qualifier**, that a player must have five unpaired cards of 8 or less to win the low end of the pot. If no player has an 8-or-better qualifier, then the best high hand scoops the pot. For example, if the best low at the table is 9-6-5-4-2, then there is no qualified low hand and the best high hand wins the entire pot. The best high and low hand can be held by the same player; if so, that player also **scoops**. This version of seven-card stud high-low is called **seven-card stud high-low 8-or-better**, or simply, **seven-card stud 8-or better**.